SURVIVING
RELIGION

SURVIVING RELIGION

A PERSONAL JOURNEY OF OVERCOMING CHURCH OFFENSES AND WOUNDS

JAMES JONES

XULON PRESS

Xulon Press
2301 Lucien Way #415
Maitland, FL 32751
407.339.4217
www.xulonpress.com

xulon
PRESS

© 2020 by James Jones

All rights reserved solely by the author. The author guarantees all contents are original and do not infringe upon the legal rights of any other person or work. No part of this book may be reproduced in any form without the permission of the author. The views expressed in this book are not necessarily those of the publisher.

Unless otherwise indicated, Scripture quotations taken from the Holy Bible, New International Version (NIV). Copyright © 1973, 1978, 1984, 2011 by Biblica, Inc.™. Used by permission. All rights reserved.

Printed in the United States of America

Paperback ISBN-13: 978-1-6628-0127-3
Ebook ISBN-13: 978-1-6628-0128-0

ACKNOWLEDGEMENTS

Although, there are undeniably a number of people that I owe an extreme amount of gratitude to for their support and prayers over the past fifteen years; I am compelled to single out and honor a few that I am especially thankful for.

It would seem a given to acknowledge and honor God for this book and the other related books or materials. However, the significance of His involvement in this instance goes beyond merely giving Him all the glory, honor, and praise that we typically voice. God's patience with my own lengthy healing process from the events experienced while serving in ministry allowed me to heal properly and fully. He also allowed me to refrain (if not kept me) from attempting to complete or publish these works until I was fully restored and ready. Any less of a timeline than what He allowed for me to heal would have undoubtedly resulted in written pieces that would be still laden with bitterness, anger and hurt. Allowing me to fully heal and resolve all wound also restored the hope and possibility of an eventual return to ministry.

I truly owe no other person more than I do my wife Susan of almost forty years who has provided me with more love and support than I am deserving of. She did not give up on me throughout all the pain and all the years that it has taken for both of us to heal from past wounds. Especially, when she received a lot of pressure from many family members and friends during the most trying times of our marriage to simply give up and leave our marriage. I am grateful for her courage in truly seeking God's will for our marriage and future life despite the periods of pain it would inevitably invite, rather than simply entertaining the advice and opinions of others. She persevered and believed in me when others so easily abandoned me. She has always been a human channel for helping me to hear and consider the voice of the Holy Spirit.

I want to especially thank Pastors Rory and Char Cobbs. They have a seemingly rare ability to balance love and encouragement without avoiding the difficult task of delivering the painful truth when it is needed. Their unwavering support and investment into our lives when it was needed most was nothing short of the epitome of Christ like behavior. They were such a key component in helping to initiate and perpetuate the restoration process in our marriage and our lives. Many pastors and leaders would benefit tremendously from applying their approaches on how to appropriately (and successfully) counsel during difficult times. Without their love, support, and genuineness; this book and other related works would not have been possible.

ABOUT THE AUTHOR

Jim Jones has been a leader, educator, and teacher for over 30 years. He has a Master's Degree (MA) in Communication from Bellevue University, a Bachelor's Degree (BS) in Human & Family Development from Grace University and graduate study in Counseling. He is an evangelist in the Church and is affiliated with World Bible Way Fellowship. He and his wife, Susan are partners of Surviving Religion Ministries. He is also an adjunct professor in the field of Communication Studies. He has filled a variety of roles and positions within ministry including associate pastor, evangelist, teaching, youth ministry, restoration ministry, foster care, prison/jail ministries and outreach. He has also held numerous positions outside of the church that includes experience in corporate training, adjunct professor, human services, group homes and higher education. Working both inside and outside of the Church has helped him to develop a more well-rounded background and balanced perspective across both spectrums. This book outlines his personal journey through ministry and those experiences that he and his wife encountered along the way.

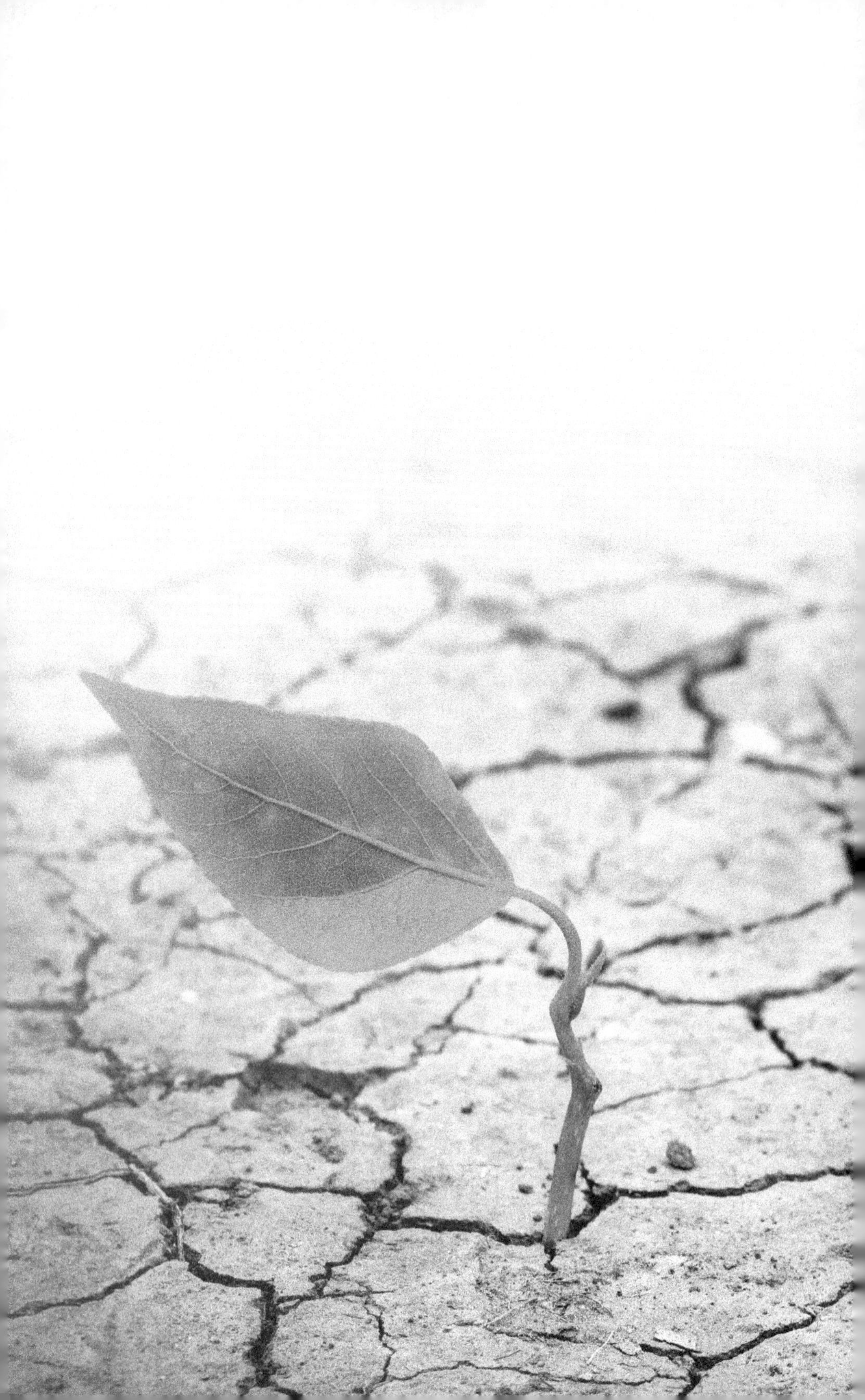

CONTENTS

Acknowledgments v
Introduction xi
Chapter 1   Believe me; I know 1
Chapter 2   A Cracked but Firm Foundation 13
Chapter 3   Living a Lifestyle of Least Resistance 27
Chapter 4   Call to Ministry. 45
Chapter 5   The Early Challenges in Ministry 67
Chapter 6   Wonder Years. 89
Chapter 7   The Good, the Bad and the Ugly 109
Chapter 8   Pride Goes Before Destruction. 133
Chapter 9   The Unpardonable Sin. 145
Chapter 10 On the Road to Restoration 167
Conclusion 179
Endnotes. 187

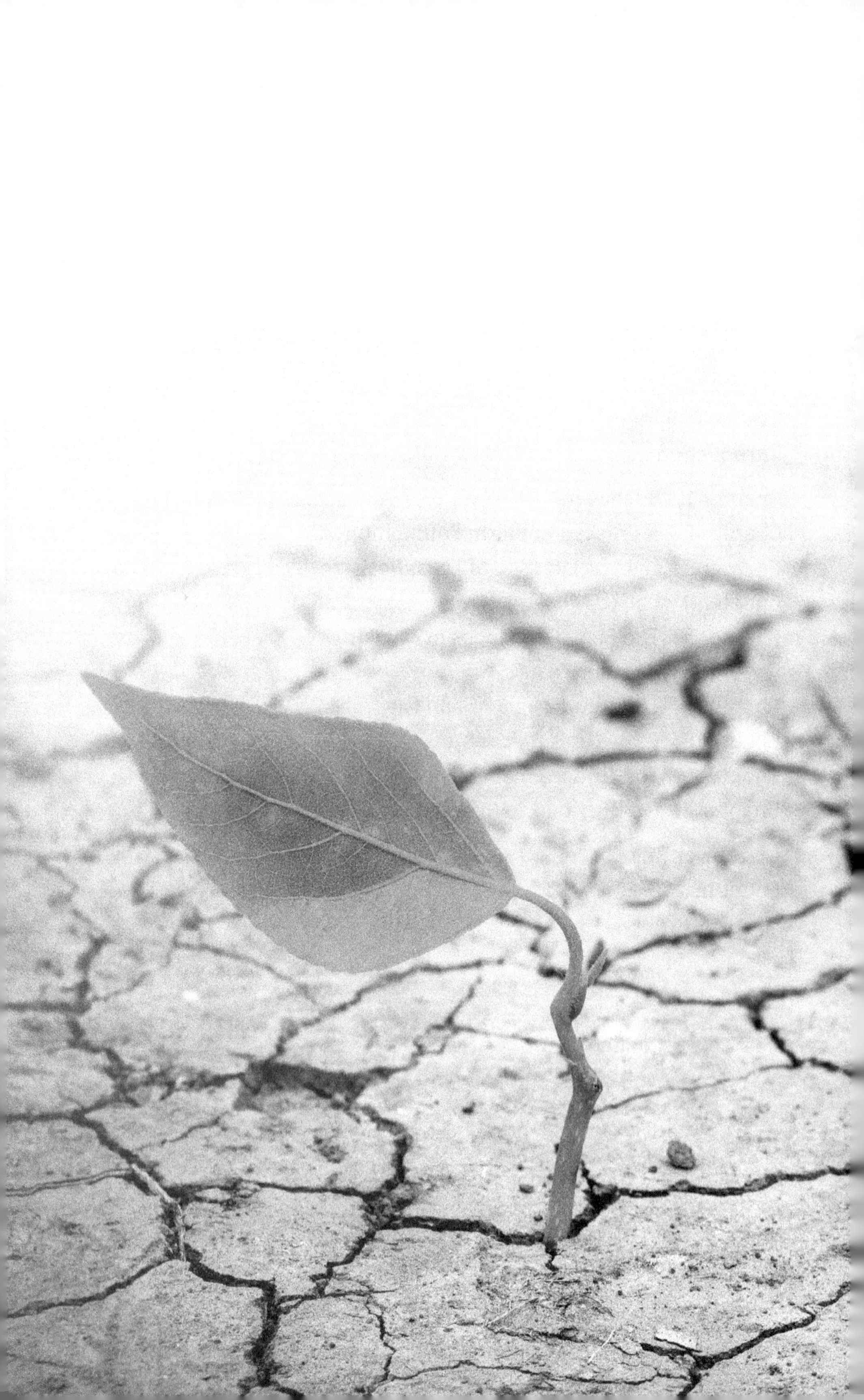

INTRODUCTION

This book is part of a small series related to the topic of surviving church offenses and healing the wounds caused by them. It is the more personal backstory and origin of the compelling need for addressing the problems associated with church offenses and wounds. This book evolved out of the necessity to separate the more personal association with church offenses from the practical and deeper teaching components found in this book's counterpart, *Surviving Religion: How religion is hurting the church*. Although each book can stand upon its own purpose and can easily be read independently of one another; I am sure that you will find that they uniquely complement one another.

Each chapter in this book provides an important part of the story of my lifelong association and relationship with the church. That relationship includes a portrait of my experiences both inside and outside of the church, which have clearly contributed to who I am today. The book reveals many of the challenges and early experiences that my wife and I encountered while serving in ministry. Unknowingly, any of those experiences were spiritually injurious at the time and ultimately led to an accumulation of damaging church hurts.

Initially, I set out with the vision of writing just one book that would effectively address the issues associated with church offenses and wounds. The vision was with a two-fold purpose: one purpose was to help bring healing to those who had experienced damaging church offenses and the other was to help the churches identify and correct areas of behaviors that all too often are the cause(s) of the offenses. However, the farther along that I got in the process, the more I realized (with insight from my wife and the Holy Spirit) that there was a need to actually construct two separate books with different, albeit very closely related uses.

On one hand this book is like a personal testimony that is intended to help or relate to anyone with similar past circumstances; and yet, it is also designed to be a valid and effective launching pad for its deeper counterpart. I firmly believe that this personal account of our experiences in ministry allows me to not only speak profoundly about the topic of church offenses and wounds; but, also helps to establish a level of ministerial credibility that supports the teachings and practical implications offered in my other books.

This personal narrative would seem like a short book when you stop to consider that it encompasses nearly sixty years of my life. However, the goal was not to write an autobiography or even a complete testimony, but rather to illustrate how our early life influences and bad experiences in the church are deeply related to church offenses or wounds. This personal account is strategically if not tactically intended to relate, identify, and bond with a large population of people that have also been impacted by church offenses.

The first chapter of the book provides a brief overview of how church offenses are causing lasting spiritual wounds in people and simultaneously crippling the church. The overview is not extensive. It is an intentionally scaled down since my premise of the negative impact that church offenses have on the church body and our churches is more deeply and sufficiently provided in the teaching counterpart to this book.

The next few chapters in the early part of the book seek to lay a foundation to the journey by revealing the dynamics involved with my upbringing, homelife and my longstanding but somewhat tumultuous relationship with the church. I am certain that this foundation and my experiences will be helpful in illustrating both the lengthy and deep association that I have had with the church as well as its impact upon my life. Those chapters include a depiction of the many influences in my life that led to my own personal exodus or drifting away from the church for a time. They also include a contrasting time period where God's patience, grace, and mercy are on full display with my eventual return to the church and ultimately a call to ministry.

This book then transitions to a partially detailed account of some of the ministries and church positions that my wife and I were associated with or called to. Our time(s) in ministry could easily and accurately be described as "the good, the bad and the ugly." My own personal encounters in ministry were strikingly similar to a host of biblical personalities. From the call and negative experiences of Jeremiah; to the ups and downs of Paul the Apostle; and, even the maltreatment from religious leaders that was not all that much unlike what Jesus had faced.

The last few chapters of the book give a detailed account of some of the most agonizing personal trials that my wife and I faced in our marriage and in our time in ministry. Quite frankly, it was also the most difficult time in my life. It was a period of time where our marriage was in serious jeopardy and ministry came to a screeching halt due to a moral failure on my part. The abrupt halt and time of necessary healing would unexpectedly take nearly fifteen years before a "full" restoration and return to ministry was finally realized. That lengthy time frame for healing was largely related to the effects of the extremely damaging church wounds incurred through my fall in ministry. To be honest; there were many times where I did not know if I would ever make it back. Or, if I even really wanted to.

The very end of the book takes a final quick turn. However, this instance is towards the good or positive path of restoration. And, once again it is a clear demonstration of God's patience, grace, mercy, faithfulness, forgiveness, and love displayed in our lives. It includes a high-level view of the steps or necessary components for healing from damaging church wounds. A more in-depth, researched, and extensive look into the healing process can be found in the other book of the series that I mentioned which is designed for that purpose.

My prayer for anyone reading this book (or its counterpart) is that you will obtain whatever healing from any church wounds that is needed, and you will reclaim the joy of the Lord by returning to church, serving others, and connecting with the rest of the Church body. Everyone is of vital importance to the church body and that includes their physical presence and interaction with the other members. Church health is dependent upon overcoming the deception that you can successfully fulfill your Christian walk alone and then coming to the realization that................. *"you do indeed need the church; and the church needs you!"*

1
BELIEVE ME; I KNOW

I acknowledge that there are some if not many books and resources available that seek to address the issue of church offenses. But I believe that the vast majority of them are tremendously insufficient for successfully addressing the entire topic of church offenses. Some resources talk about church offenses, but they do not offer very much help or consideration towards the church wounds that were caused by them. Nor do they sufficiently address the impact to the church overall if they even make note of it in the least bit. Other books or resources talk about the church wounds, but they fall tremendously if not irresponsibly short in offering anything substantive about the actual offenses being perpetrated in the church.

Many churches seem to be comfortable or satisfied with being a spiritual triage unit that occasionally offers a spiritual healing series and errantly thinks that is all that is needed for addressing the issue. It begs the question, "do they not know, or do they just not care?" Does it seem futile to them to even think about trying to change things in our churches today that might actually reduce the number of church offenses? Why would any church leader want to continue down this circular path that brings them back to the same place over and over again? For years, I have tried to figure out whether it was spiritual blindness, pure ignorance, incapable leadership, spiritual immaturity, lack of ministerial experience, or even apathy that allows church offenses to continue with little opposition or evidence of churches trying to eradicate them. Perhaps, it is a combination of those factors?

I am quite certain that a huge part of the equation or reason for their inability to effectively address church offenses and church wounds is that many current pastors and leaders are not able to look at this issue objectively and honestly from both perspectives. They have either not experienced the damaging potential of a church wound or they have forgotten what it was like to experience them when they began ministry and now enjoy a more "protected" status. And, of course when you consider that they are part of the population who are most likely to cause those offenses; you shouldn't expect too many of them to all of a sudden realize their own personal failure in addressing church wounds unless it is illuminated and brought to their attention.

Sadly, I would contend that nearly all of them (if not all) of the pastors, leaders, churches, books and resources that have tried to publicly address this particular subject; have overlooked or underestimated the tremendous impact that church wounds inflict upon the body of Christ and the churches. For example, they have failed to consider that those offenses just might have rendered a wounded person sitting in the pews as useless when it comes to serving or engaging in the church. Yes, they attend regularly but what value are they bringing (e.g. serving, building community, spiritually growing, etc.). I do not say that judgingly against the one wounded but rather as one who knows firsthand what it is like! They have also failed to grasp the gravity of the situation when they do know about someone's church wounds. They fail to sufficiently recognize that those wounds that are currently in hiding will eventually surface at perhaps the most inopportune time and will undoubtedly result in them and quite possibly others leaving the church.

Church offenses are impacting the churches and hurting the body of Christ in ways that far exceed someone's mere hurt feelings or the ministerial assumption that it is just part of the dynamics involved with serving in ministry. I am tempted to even go so far as to say that they are crippling if not destroying the Church. Church offenses and their subsequent wounds impact the lives of those who have been hurt, those who are closely related to them, those who shepherd or minister to them and the church they might call home. Their home church is negatively impacted regardless of whether the church is involved with the offense or not. Ultimately, the damaging impact will no doubt evolve into their own exodus from the church altogether if the wounds are not resolved or reconciled to a point that allows restoration.

I believe that most people who have left the church would have preferred to remain a part of it and the community that it jointly offers. I am certain that most people who have been hurt through bad church experiences would like to still have access to God, but want to be able to do so without having to relive the bad experiences they went through while serving in ministry or attending church. Even if our own actions were possibly part of what initiated or invited those offenses in the first place. My own personal story included in this book details my fall in ministry and the related church wounds associated with that personal disaster. Although it is traumatic, devastating and certainly not something that you would want to wish upon anyone else; those experiences have enabled me to understand and relate to many other people who have faced or are facing the same challenges. Despite the unfortunate, painful, and even disastrous consequences for me at the time; God is now using it to benefit many of you.

Yes, I painfully know what it is like to want to still enjoy God's presence but at the same time having a desire to do so without the painful reminder(s) of past church wounds. Or, living with the dreaded possibility of encountering the people who might have initiated the church offenses. I am all too familiar with succumbing to the irresistible temptations that deceivingly convince you that you can somehow avoid any remembrance of the offense by simply not attending church or at least hiding somewhere among the congregation.

Hiding sounds good, and to be honest with you it actually "feels" good for a while because of the reduced level of vulnerability, fear, and pain that you have to deal with. At least temporarily anyway. However, the problem with the falsehood associated with "hiding" is that you gain a fake sense of still being able to connect with God in an unfettered way. You become spiritually persuaded by the enemy that your relationship with God is unhindered. What you really need to understand though is that those wounds or offenses are still impacting you negatively in some way and they will prevent you from going any deeper than the weak level of trust that you currently have.

I have included numerous personal experiences and examples in this book that detail real life incidences that my wife and I encountered and endured throughout ministry. Many of those experiences will likely resonate in varying degrees with some if not all of you. Though sharing any portion of a testimony can instantly make someone vulnerable; I believe that the value it will bring in this instance goes beyond my own personal risks that I face. A lot of what I share on the personal level would likely be extremely difficult for most people to reveal about their personal life. I am sure of that because it required "years" of careful and prayerful consideration just for me to be able to share many of the details.

As an evangelist and pastor, I have worked with personal testimonies most of my life and I know how powerful they can be. But I also know what a delicate situation it is. Sharing personal life experiences automatically raises the level of vulnerability for the individual and even their family members. I have seen way too many instances where someone's testimony had become the fodder for gossip or used against them in some way. Nonetheless, I firmly believe that examples or stories that I have included in this book are critical towards helping you to develop a more thorough if not personal understanding of church offenses. And, they should also clearly indicate my unique ability or expertise to effectively address this issue.

Despite my desire to be as transparent as possible there will be a bit of a restraint on my part to offer only those details deemed necessary in getting the point across. I did not feel that mentioning everything or providing more graphic details was necessary or advisable in some instances. Nor did I feel it beneficial in any way to personally identify specific churches, affiliated denominations, or anyone specifically who have brought offenses upon us. I have been able to heal from those wounds without having to name or exploit any of the individuals or organizations that are mentioned. I am confident that the descriptions provided will be more than enough for understanding the general idea of the examples given and still effectively connect to many folks that can relate to my life experiences.

You should also keep in mind as you make your way through the book that even though the events or observations of the church that I have presented are a true and accurate account; the examples given to you exist upon their own merits and circumstances. In other words, regardless of how prevalent a particular issue might be within the church or what you might also have experienced; it is not necessarily representative of what everyone should expect to encounter or see in every church. No church is perfect and church offenses (both legitimate offenses and perceived offenses) undoubtedly happen in every church. I cannot see the possibility of any church being completely free of them when considering that the Church is made up of individual human beings or people and thus it is inherently subject to inaccuracies, disagreement, mistakes, flawed perceptions, and even wrongful behavior.

Though, I can attest to the widespread incidences of church hurts, it is vitally important to point out that my wife and I have also spent many years in a variety of ministries, churches and roles that were both enjoyable and fruitful while clearly being absent of an overwhelming spirit of religion. Those ministries and churches all made a strong ongoing and consistent effort to try and exhibit true Christ like character that created an environment less likely to causing serious or perpetual offenses. The memory and number of those wonderful experiences undoubtedly were powerful factors towards helping us to overcome past church hurts and keeping me and my wife from the temptations to abandon or leave the Church.

That being said, despite all the wonderful and fruitful experiences that take place in church or serving in ministry; church offenses or wounds are sadly still commonplace in the church today. Unfortunately, a lot of people who experience church offenses do not have the foundation, history, fortitude, support, determination, or spiritual maturity that my wife and I had at the time that we either encountered or had to deal with them. The fact that many people have been wrongfully "pushed" or "forced" out of the church has weighed heavy on my heart over the years and its importance has compelled me to finally speak out and write about it.

Why, is it such an important issue? Because it has kept so many people from attending church regularly. For many people who might still attend church but are carrying the baggage of unresolved church offenses through the doors when they come; it severely hinders their spiritual growth and level of commitment to the church. That negatively impacts the health of the church despite any intention to do so or not. Though they are attending church, they are still isolated in a way which typically keeps them from serving regularly in the church or experiencing a level of community that they could and should be enjoying. And ultimately, their hidden wounds will affect others around them.

The hurt, pain, anger, and bitterness caused by church offenses have convinced many people to seek alternative venues to connect with God apart from congregating with others. Opting instead for online services, external Bible groups or simply drifting away from any connection to the Church body altogether. Those alternative options to attending church regularly are commonly accepted or should I say "positively spun" in Christian circles as great solutions or opportunities to reach even more people outside the church walls. Many church leaders seem to have the mindset or perspective that those people using alternative options rather than personally attending church are a new or supplemental population to their own congregation or regular attendees. However, in reality a great deal of those people utilizing alternative resources actually represent the population that has left the church and most likely will even become further separated as time goes on.

Church leaders, pastors, Christian publications, and other voices in the Christian community have joyously and sometimes blindly welcomed all the technological advances and new online resources available as viable, convenient, and acceptable alternatives. As an evangelist, I understand the thought processes and excitement regarding the potential for reaching a new and an even larger audience in ways that were never before available. Admittedly there are some undeniable positive uses as well as some extraordinary opportunities for people to access God in various ways outside of the church walls with today's technology. But it is not without dangers or cost as it should never come at the expense of coming together as a church community to worship and fellowship together. That cost or absence from the Church body affects both the individual and the Church body as a whole.

I am convinced that the after effect or fallout of church offenses has largely contributed to the number of people remaining outside of the church walls and particularly those who once attended but now choose to look for other ways to spiritually connect outside of attending church. The significance and the contribution that church offenses have on the decline in church attendance has seemingly been given little consideration if not completely ignored. I do not believe that too many other people (if any) beyond myself have taken the time lately to address church offenses as the primary or even a major contributor. Yet, attendance numbers for the church have continuously declined since early 1970's and it appears to be almost unstoppable as it continues to decline.

Church leaders and researchers for decades now have looked at other reasons or ways to combat the decline in church attendance including cultural shift, changing styles or preferences of worship, generational priorities, facilities, amenities, programs or even doctrinal positions. Despite the well-intentioned changes to these areas of the church over the years, none of them have proven to sufficiently alter the trend. And yet, in the wake of numerous or major changes to the church programs and amenities lies the past investment. All alone and without a solution to the church exodus, which at a minimum suggests our thoughts about the cause for a declining church attendance must have missed the mark.

Many of the changes to church functions or services thought to inhibit or limit church growth were arguably still necessary and perhaps even essential. Some have even undeniably helped to improve the church atmosphere or health in many ways. However, even cumulatively those positive changes have still not stopped the ongoing exodus of the church ranks. Churches have continually chased after the seemingly unattainable goal of trying to meet people's revolving needs. Their thinking and actions were based on the hope that eventually they might come up with the right formula to maintain church vitality and growth and stop the migration or departure from the church.

People have unfortunately and yet effectively been deceived into believing that they do not have a "real need" to physically attend church any longer in spite of all those efforts by the church to heighten the appeal. Unresolved past church offenses have inconspicuously served to reinforce the belief that attendance is insignificant or unnecessary for a strong Christian walk. That belief has alarmingly boosted the population of those outside the church walls. And, as if declining church attendance were not a big enough concern in itself; church offenses also cripple many individuals within the church. They may not have left the church altogether just yet, but they are disconnected in many ways and are not actually serving in the church because of some past offense that has yet to be reconciled.

I have personally learned over the years that overcoming church offenses (and particularly when serving in ministry) is something that many people have been unable to easily address or conquer on their own. The offenses can be difficult to overcome and many of them take a long time to heal from. They can cause or invite other problems like mental health issues, anger management, financial woes, bitterness, resentment, relationship issues and many other worrisome behaviors. Of course, the spiritual hindrances and impact are the primary concern; but the practical daily life impact on an individual should also be of concern to those who pastor or lead these wounded individuals. The enemy of our soul wants to destroy people and our dismissal or failure to recognize all implications or areas of attack is part of his scheme to go beyond the individual person and destroy your church as well.

The damaging impact that church offenses have on the Church and on other individuals besides myself became an important part of the concern that I developed over the years and the motivation for this written work. It goes way beyond just my own personal experiences. Even though the examples and stories in this book are primarily of a personal nature, I know that church offenses are not exclusive to just me and my wife. Sadly, I have discovered that they have proven to be more frequent and widespread than many people and church leaders appear to think that they are. This period of indifference or at least spiritual oblivion has caused considerable damage to the health of the Church body, declining church attendance and even the exodus of those serving in ministry.

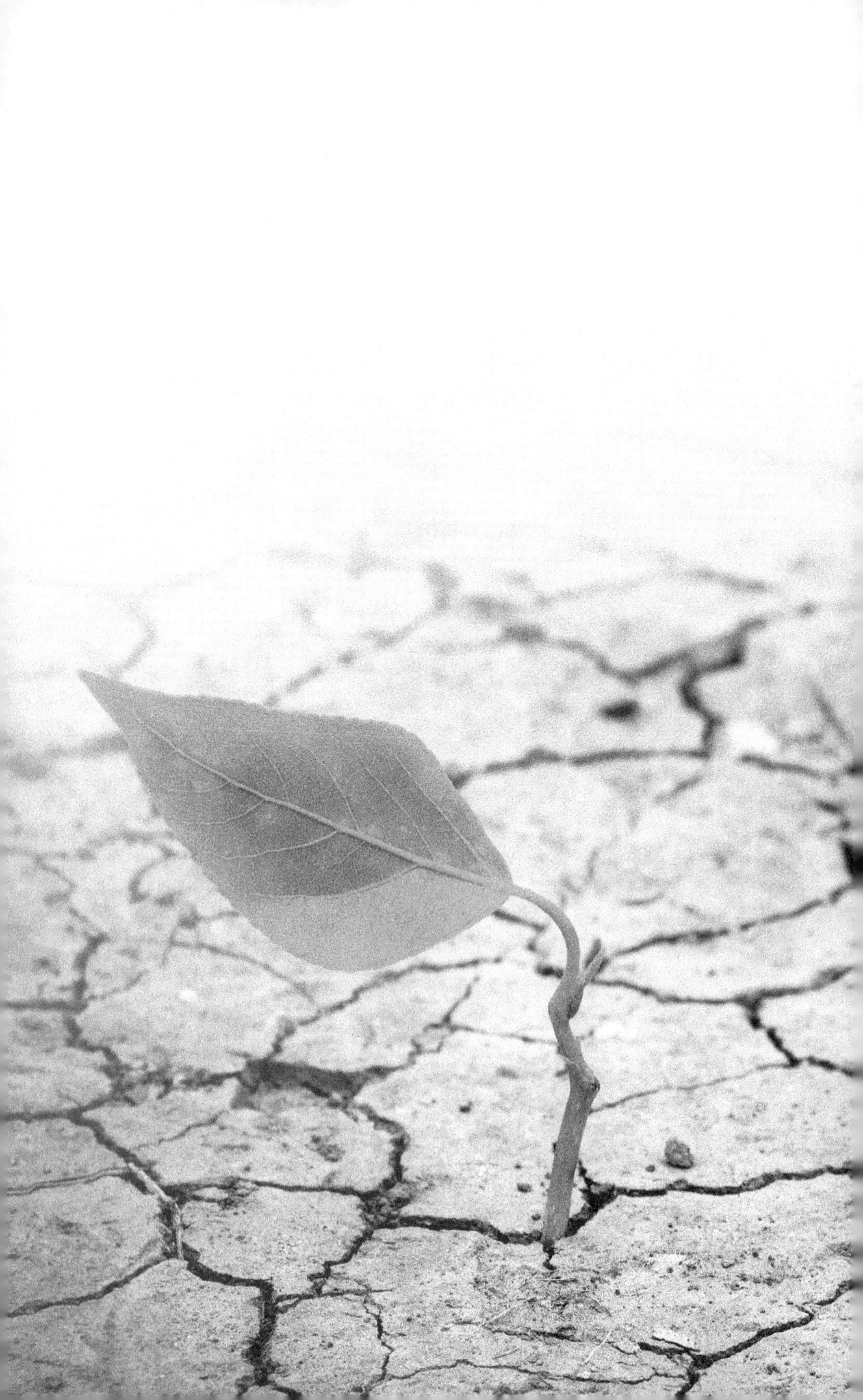

2
A CRACKED BUT FIRM FOUNDATION

*"Train up a child in the way he should go,
And when he is old he will not depart from it."*
Proverbs 22:6 NKJ

During my early childhood and teen years back in the 1960's and 1970's; families on the average were quite a bit more stable in their marriages and households than today. Divorce was not entirely non-existent, but it was certainly much rarer than it has grown to be in the last few decades. It was even more rare for folks to remarry more than once if they remarried at all. That was no doubt a good thing considering the impact that divorce has on families and more specifically on the children.

During that time most young people had to wait until high school or college to actually know what the word "dysfunction" meant. However, I grew up learning about it at a much earlier age. My parents were married and divorced to other people an unbelievable ten times combined. My dad was married and divorced six times and my mom four times. You can do the math and figure out how many different stepdads and stepmoms I must have had over the years. And, maybe you can even try to imagine what that might have been like for me and my siblings.

It would not seem like this type of an environment would have been one in which going to church was a priority, and it probably would not have been were it not for my grandmother. She was a committed churchgoer and a godly woman that exemplified perhaps the most valuable standard and example for my life. I still have a vivid recollection of her starting every day at the kitchen table opening her Bible and praying before starting any of her daily tasks. Her undeterred insistence that we attend church forced our parents to drop us off at church every Sunday when we were younger though they themselves did not attend. Ensuring that we went to church each week proved to be beneficial by not only providing us with a reprieve from a chaotic and oftentimes abusive home environment; but more importantly it exposed us to God and the church at an early age. This was a key if not essential time in my life. The Bible says "train a child in the way he should go, and when he is old he will not turn from it." This would prove to be a profoundly if not prophetically true statement in my life when I left the church for a period of time and eventually found my way back. I am convinced that it holds true for others as well.

Although, I would eventually fade away from regular church attendance for a short period in my life as a young adult; I must admit that in my early years I was fortunate enough to experience a lot of good things that were meaningful and would stay with me throughout my life. Things like Sunday School, Royal Rangers, Youth Group, and people who genuinely loved me and gave me more attention, stability, and love than I was getting at home. Those programs or ministries also helped to provide an early basic Christian education that filled an empty spiritual void. A void that existed because it was not being provided at home. And of utmost importance was the fact that the Pentecostal church was where I first gave my life to Jesus. Even though I really did not "fully" understand what that meant or the significance of it at my early age; it would ultimately prove to be the most significant and important point in my life.

The churches I attended back then were mainly Pentecostal or charismatic churches and because of that they naturally provided an environment that exposed me to great worship music, dynamic preaching and an evangelistic emphasis that would lay a foundation for the path I took in ministry years later. Those experiences also instilled a love and respect for the church that even the biggest of flaws or church hurts would not be able to erase years later. Those church services I attended were much different and much longer than they are today.

Some of you may struggle with a service that goes beyond an hour or even an hour and fifteen minutes, but church for me while growing up oftentimes was an all Sunday event. It began with Sunday School in the morning and then regular church service afterwards. There may have been one or two church services to attend depending on the size of the church. For our denomination this would typically be followed by a potluck lunch, afternoon fellowship or games for the young people and then a Sunday evening service. It did not bother us or seem like an inconvenience on our schedule to spend an entire Sunday at church. It seemed quite normal to spend time with the community of believers instead of just dutifully attending one service on Sundays.

So, lest you be tempted to think that I have long-standing issues with the church in general or a critical attitude as you make your way through my *Surviving Religion* books merely because I address some difficult topics; you might well be reminded that my background is deeply rooted in the church environment and that I actually have a deep love for it. I love worship, I love the Word, I love good preaching or teaching, and I love the people. What I do not love is when the Christian life is reduced to mere religion or religious practices and becomes the source for pain or hurts in individuals. I have been involved with it long enough to know the difference.

Unfortunately, though as a young teen I was slowly being pulled into a direction away from the church despite my early upbringing. I was not unlike many other teens or young adults that also did not have a homelife capable of consistently reinforcing the values and teachings of the church. My parents entered into one relationship after another and we were constantly having to "choose" between one household over the other. They sought allegiance from each of us through contentious and never-ending custody battles which resulted in even more conflict, divisiveness and dysfunction between me and my siblings that exists in many ways still to this day. It was extremely difficult to sort out as a young person. I often wondered, "How could a home environment that was abusive, chaotic, and not at all like what they talked about in church support the church's contention that God cared about you or was actively involved in your life?"

Although, I have never doubted the significance or reality of my salvation; it should not come as a complete surprise to some people that I easily got further and further away from leading a good Christian life. Over time I also developed a waning desire to attend church any longer. It is difficult to stay on track as a young person while dealing with family conflict or dysfunction in the home on a regular if not daily basis. I can assure you that it was extremely challenging in my life to face it on a continual basis and trust me when I say that it is "not something that you would want to be around if you could avoid it." It is an even worse situation when you are forced to endure things like physical abuse as I was exposed to on a regular basis. Without going into specific details, I can tell you that it went well beyond the culturally acceptable mere spankings or "whooping's" that many of you might have also experienced. Pretty tough to see God's love in all of that!

Even yet today, I still do not think that people fully understand or grasp the gravity of how divorce impacts the children. Divorce has become increasingly more frequent if not commonplace in our society and it has been seemingly accepted in modern culture as an event that is somewhat normal or to be expected. Especially in American culture. Society tends to emphasize the negative impact that divorce has on the adults involved with, instead of focusing on the possibly more impacting and lifetime effect it has on the children. As a young person who experienced divorce many times; I can tell you that it is much easier and more appealing to spend time with your friends and out on the streets. Those places at least provide opportunities for you to escape your world rather than deal with a dysfunctional home environment all the time. Because of that opportunity to escape and enjoy some periods of peace in my childhood; I spent most of my junior high and high school years intentionally avoiding the atmosphere of my own household and family.

Both of my parents were preoccupied with their own interests and new relationships (not to mention constantly fighting with one another) so, they did not really seem to care too much that I was practically never at home. My absence was typically under the auspices that I was "staying over" at a friend's house; but in reality... I was practically living in their homes more so than just spending the night or weekend. I stayed or lived with my best friend's family most of the time. In some ways, his family virtually adopted me. They knew about my disruptive homelife, so their hospitality extended beyond just providing a place to hang out or perhaps stay over for the weekend. I had my own dresser, my own bed, regular chores, and I even went on family vacations with them. They treated me as if I were just another member of their large family.

Because I was hardly ever at home, I no longer regularly attended a Pentecostal or Protestant church with my grandmother or siblings. However, I was required to attend Catholic mass every week. My best friend's family was Catholic and basically it was expected of me since I was staying in their home and considered "one of the family." The Catholic church did not do much for me spiritually. It did however introduce me to another aspect or perspective on how to live a "religious" lifestyle. One that puts a lot of merit on regular attendance and going through the right motions as if that is somehow enough for living a true Christian life.

It was okay with me having the requirement to attend mass, as I had grown up with a church environment anyway and one that had much higher expectations for church involvement. I did not really understand too much about all the denominational differences back then anyway, so the judgmental evaluation of Catholicism never really came into play for me at that time. In hindsight I do owe them for at least incorporating something religious into my life during that period. Who knows what my life would have looked like without at least that little bit of religious input and influence into my life? Unfortunately, though, it lacked in any true spiritual experience for me personally and it only ended up contributing to the reasons for me growing further away from the Church and ultimately questioning its relevancy later on.

I would discover many years later as an evangelist and through the thousands of encounters I had with people, just how many of them like myself have been deceived into thinking that a little bit of religion on the surface was somehow sufficient or meaningful. Many of us were taught back then that simply identifying as a Christian or proclaiming that you believe in God is somehow adequate for maintaining any power over your lifestyle. Many people today still believe that merely belonging to a church will somehow be enough to give you the necessary will and fortitude of resisting the daily temptations that this world has to offer.

Though the Catholic church and some of the new non-denominational churches that offer a much laxer perspective on what it means to be a Christian, are the ones who typically are blamed as being steeped in "religion" rather than relationship with Jesus Christ: I have found it to be a rampant problem in many of the Christian denominations and churches. Countless numbers of people over the years have been fooled into believing that occasional participation in religious activities like "just going to church", "being baptized", "taking communion" or "confessing your guilt" once in a while will somehow compensate for your recent sins or misdeeds and sufficiently keep you from straying too far from your Christian principles. That has been a message conveyed or propagated by many denominations and religions. Not just the Catholic church. Many of us were being led to believe that it is as easy as admitting that even though you might not be a "good" Christian or a practicing one; you are still a Christian. But, I learned over the years that this perspective really is a view that errantly confuses or mixes up the different issues between our salvation and living a Christian lifestyle.

Those are two separate and deep theological topics that go well beyond the scope of this book. So, let me just simply say that the emphasis here is not on whether you lose your salvation or not (if you indeed made a serious commitment to Jesus at some point) but rather on the deception that mere church attendance, religious activities or casual belief in God can somehow give you the power to lead a good Christian life. They can be good practices or disciplines, but they cannot give you any power over your everyday life. Sadly, those false beliefs obscure reality as you fail to acknowledge how your life gets farther and farther away from its spiritual foundation until it no longer resembles anything like a Christian lifestyle. Typically, it is a slow and subtle if not almost unnoticeable change over time that works against the principles and standards you had embraced. Bit by bit the lines you have drawn or swore you would never cross are moved or even erased and you find yourself doing things that you promised you would never do or engage in.

All too often when a young person ends up not having any continuous spiritual guidance or support as they grow up; it tends to lead them toward the experimentation or abuse of drugs and alcohol. The likelihood of this no doubt increases if they come from a troubled home environment as they seek ways to fill the empty voids or escape reality. Although, drug and alcohol use or abuse has continued to increase in our nation's population over the years; it is arguably less likely or pervasive for someone that is living under the protection or scrutiny that a normal household would provide. Especially, if that home had had some level of spiritual guidance as well.

The lack of supervision or accountability in my life allowed me to get away with things that I might not otherwise have been able to inconspicuously hide. Or, at least not on such a regular basis anyway. It was not the fault of the Catholic family that I lived with. Even though they treated me like one of their family members (including disciplining me as necessary), there was only so much that they could do. I still spent a lot of time away from them as I occasionally drifted back and forth between their home and whatever parent's household that I was supposed to be growing up in. It was an inconsistent and fractured lifestyle that they were not really responsible for, despite their willingness to still care for me well beyond what my parents or anyone else did. Unfortunately, they just could not consistently provide the same level of accountability or oversight that a spiritual environment can. One that exposes or brings to light what is really going on in your children's lives. So, because of the awkward situation where I went back and forth between households; I still pretty much went and did as I pleased.

In my teenage years I spent a lot of my time "partying", skipping school and other juvenile delinquent behavior. I was able to largely escape the suspicion of any existing problem (criminal or otherwise) by creating a facade that looked like I was involved with regular or normal young adult activities like anyone else. In other words, most people would have thought I was largely living a normal teenage life with just a few occasional bumps along the road. I participated regularly in sports and engaged in all the other normal social or scholastic activities that young people took part in. I did exceptionally well in school in most subjects and oftentimes was even at the top of my class. At least until a later downward slide would catch up to me when my lack of interest and underachievement became more noticeable.

Over time my desire or motivations to excel in things like school or sports started to decrease. I did just enough work at school and avoided drawing too much attention to myself by eluding any major issues like being awarded long suspensions or getting kicked out of school altogether. The few incidences or run ins with the law (on the rare occasions that I got caught) were typically thought of as just normal childhood boundary testing at the time. No one seemed to suspect that I had any issues (particularly spiritual) outside of what they would expect for any young person that might come from my background or circumstances.

I was generally considered a smart young man; however, it was a given that my performance was not reflective of my intelligence level or capabilities. I just had other interests shall I say. Regrettably, I did not have much desire or motivation to make those capabilities work to my advantage that would allow me to capitalize on my intelligence, abilities, or potential back then. Primarily, because partying and being "cool" or well-liked was somewhat appealing to me. I had little parental involvement to provide the necessary correction or convince me otherwise. However, I was still smart enough on my own to figure out that I needed to complete at least minimal amounts of work or sufficiently meet some level of expectation if I wanted to escape suspicion or speculation about what was really going on in my life.

Some would argue that it was not being smart at all and instead it was rather manipulative, deceitful, or conniving. They would be right to a certain degree, yet it still takes a level of intelligence or "smarts" to be good at it or at least go undetected for the most part. And, I learned to be very good at it. I was calm and convincing under pressure. Hard to read. Good at lying with a straight face. A salesman of sorts. Being a "cool customer" as some called it. I found great success in being able to fool others and thus I avoided getting caught in more bad deeds than I care to mention. Obviously, now as an adult and in hindsight it is at the very least saddening and regrettable that I did not use my skills and abilities in the right ways. Those laudable traits could have helped me to experience success in my life at a much earlier stage in life than I did if I would have only taken advantage of them. I could have avoided many of the consequences and challenges that I went through unnecessarily in my young adult life.

Unfortunately, I also did not have the necessary support systems and family stability in place that no doubt would have helped me to resist some of the peer pressure and temptations of a harmful lifestyle. It is obvious that God carefully designed the family structure for good reason as there are unavoidable consequences for families or individuals operating outside of the ideal (e.g. divorce, pregnancy out of wedlock, etc.). Some of you may not like hearing me say this because you happen to be in one of those situations and may be sensitive to these subjects (e.g. you're a single mom, you got pregnant at an early age, you're remarried, etc.). You might be having an emotional reaction or level of defensiveness just because I even mention it. Or, you might feel like it is an attack on any personal accomplishments that you have made in overcoming those scenarios in your life.

I don't bring this area of discussion up to cause offense or for the sake of judging anyone; however, it is important that you realize that although God is loving and forgiving it does not dismiss the truth or reality of the consequences for the choices we make in life. Some of those can even last a lifetime. Although, God can and will certainly help us deal with those consequences we cannot expect for them to just magically disappear or ignore them. I personally can attest to the impact that divorce and the lack of family structure has on young people's lives even though it is so often denied or minimized by society today. Those support systems or a strong family environment are critical to the human development, character and spiritual development of young people and you need to know that. The impact will show at some point in your life.

Let me be clear that I am not trying to blame all the poor choices that I personally have made throughout my life on other people, my parents, a tough upbringing, or even solely on the absence of a wholesome family environment. Many times, I had an opportunity to make the right choice and I knew it at the time, but I still elected to do what was wrong instead of what was right. Especially, as I got older. And, despite all the challenges while growing up, I have demonstrated in my own life (and other people have as well) that a successful and Christian lifestyle is still possible despite the absence of those critical support systems and lack of spiritual guidance. What I am pointing out is the huge importance of a strong, stable, and spiritually immersed home environment. It would have helped to sustain the passion that I had for church involvement at a younger age and arguably helped to avoid many of the temptations or being drawn to the deceptive "fun" of a secular and self-centered lifestyle.

In addition to avoiding those temptations; I believe that at least some of the church offenses that I and my family were subject to over the years might not have been as impacting or disabling as they were. I believe that a more stable and spiritually influenced upbringing would have given me some of the tools necessary for dismissing or overcoming church offenses. A strong and consistent spiritual atmosphere could have helped to develop an awareness and toughness that does not so easily succumb to psychological impairment brought on by personal attacks, maltreatment, gossip, or adversity. Although, we know that God can certainly use all things "for the good", it is not necessarily an easily accepted position for us to vocalize while we go through those difficult times. And, most of us would have no doubt preferred to learn our lessons through and easier and less painful experience.

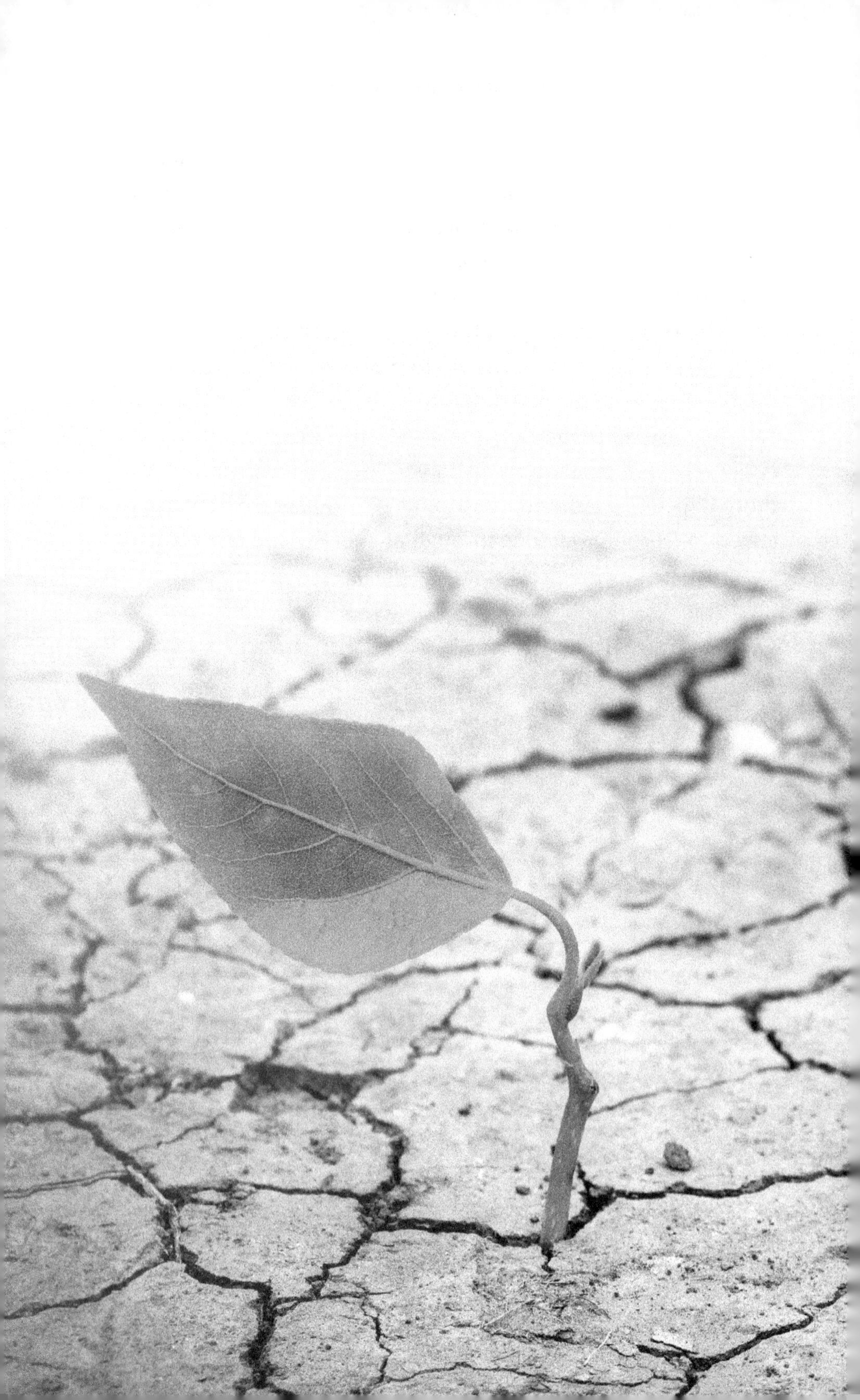

3

LIVING A LIFESTYLE OF LEAST RESISTANCE

The path of least resistance was first used by chemist Le Chatelier when discussing chemical reactions, but it has been used by many people in a lot of different contexts. It seems to me that it can be applied to how many of us live out our lives in trying to avoid conflict, stress, confrontation, personal angst, difficulty and even change, regardless of the level of change involved. Much of my late teens and early adult life decisions were carried out in this manner and a large part of the logic or reasoning for that was due to the strife and contentious upbringing that I had experienced for most of my life. I was always looking for the more easy, effortless, uncomplicated, and painless path to take. And if "fun" was involved; then all the better.

However, even all the perceived fun, independence and freedom can grow old or unfulfilling after a while. Pretty soon you need or crave something more to satisfy that appetite. If you constantly are surrounded by a dysfunctional home environment; it causes you to yearn for some type of a more long-term escape or solution than just wandering the streets. So, ultimately, I decided to leave home and join the military at the young age of seventeen to get away from my local environment. Partly to get away from the continuous family conflicts and partly to find out what it was like to discover the world on my own. I had already been on my own in a way for several years, however I would find out that this would be an entirely different level of independence and discovery.

I enlisted into the U.S. Navy against the wishes of my parents. They thought that I was not ready for something like the military due to my young age of seventeen. Nonetheless, I was determined to establish my own life or independence and their concerns seemed largely superficial or self-serving anyway. They had not really been actively involved in my life up to this point, so I felt as if their objections were nothing more than wanting to somehow still lay claim to their rite of parenthood. I guess that it was a way for them to display some level of undeserving authority over my life.

It was so easy to enlist back then since it was immediately right after the unpopular Vietnam War, and the prospect of immediate independence and escape sounded great to me. However, I did not have a clue as to what was about to happen in my life. You do not really gain the immediate freedom or independence that you thought you would merely by enlisting. You actually end up giving ownership of your life to the military. And, they will help you to clearly understand that immediately! I had no real forethought or understanding of just how fast and how much I would have to grow up in such a short amount of time.

Stepping off that recruit bus at the Naval Recruit Training Center in Orlando, Florida back then was a rude awakening for me. You discover in just a matter of minutes that your life no longer belongs to you as the government now owns you. You enter a world where someone else will tell you what to do, what to say and what to think for however many years you just enlisted for. Like practically every other young man there, I wondered "what the heck did I just get myself into?" Just hours earlier I thought I was going off on an "adventure" and instead I had just surrendered all my freedom and independence for a new lifestyle of discipline, taking orders and enjoying only the liberties that they decided to grant me. And, granting them only within their timeline or parameters of course. Whatever structure I lacked at home or in school when I was younger was just implemented in a matter of minutes.

The military is a lot different today than it was back in the 1970's. I enlisted right at the end of the Vietnam War, so most of their strict disciplinary guidelines and sometimes harsh expectations still existed. Political correctness had not yet found its way into the military, so drill instructors or superiors were able to shame and verbally abuse you to the very brink of breaking you mentally without having any fear of backlash or any charges of abuse for yelling at you or punishing you. It all fell under the guise of "training", so it was basically deemed for your own good or in your best interest. Even the most extreme punishments were imaginatively named with terms like "motivational training." Unfortunately, I had the opportunity to participate in those on more than one occasion during my time in the service. True, they could almost make you feel lower than a piece of dirt at times, but their approach did have a purpose and it was extremely effective. Effective in shaping or molding young boys (and girls) from all over the different regions and cultures of the country into young men or women that needed to make up a disciplined and unified military. And doing it in a very short amount of time.

By the way; you may wonder..."what does this have to do with church offenses?" Well, I believe that it is vitally important for you to understand some of the non-church components or influences that go into the make-up of someone who God calls into the ministry later on in life. Just as it is important or even key for you to know that David was a young freckle-faced shepherd boy that went on to be King and known as someone after God's own heart; it is also meaningful for you to know about the composition of my past and the relevancy of my early background before ministry. You cannot help but wonder about God's thinking when you look at who He called to be patriarchs, prophets, kings, disciples, and apostles in light of their flaws and personal backgrounds or characteristics. Yet, their backgrounds or personal histories were critically important. Just as they are today when He calls someone! My situation was no different as the early years of my life have no doubt contributed to my penchant and sensitivity towards identifying and calling out church offenses.

Although military training was a harsh reality for those like myself that were just being introduced to it; I feel that in many ways it is some of the best training that a young person could possibly go through. I still believe to this day that the military may be the very best place for young people (men in particular) to mature and become responsible, disciplined, and productive citizens. I know that many folks will disagree with me when I say that I believe that every young man should serve in the military. But it causes one to mature quickly and develop a level of special appreciation for this country and its liberties that cannot possibly be obtained or understood unless you have served. I know that it changed me in many ways. And, practically everyone else that I know or served with. Despite whatever your attitudes, behaviors or background was beforehand.

Yes, I understand that some people have the opinion that the military's stringent and disciplined approach can be demeaning, insensitive or even abusive at times; but I have not seen anything in my lifetime outside of a spiritual change to be more effective or expeditious in changing people's lives. Even new Christians have demonstrated a longer period of necessary ongoing discipleship because your new walk is typically not as stringent or disciplined to begin with. Perhaps one of the main reasons it is so effective is because of how much of the training is extraordinarily similar or related to many biblical principles. Concepts and values like truth, honesty, integrity, servitude, courage, self-control, honor, respect, and a host of others. Besides, many of us in the military found their tactics and pre-meditated insults to be more humorous or comical than degrading at the time (especially if it was happening to someone other than yourself!) The hassles were short lived anyway and ironically after training was over the drill instructors became likeable comrades as their job of molding us was successfully completed regardless of what it took to get us there. Though basic training was over; the installation of discipline, respect and authority would not end after training.

So, despite the challenges and questionable tactics, much was to be gained from enlisting into the military and going through the rigorous training. However, there were also numerous downsides to the military life as well. Many aspects and influences associated with the military life were not conducive to encouraging a positive or Christian lifestyle. Thus, unfortunately this period of my life would also prove to be the farthest that I have been from an active relationship with God.

When I entered the military, drug use and its availability were extremely prevalent. It was not uncommon back then for even officers to be using in some capacity. Alcohol was also extremely popular. You could legally drink at the age of seventeen if you were in the military. They also had night clubs on practically every base or government installation that made it tempting to say the least. It was not only authorized or legal; it was encouraged in many ways. Especially, if you were a sailor like I was. Quite honestly, that was part of my motivation and even unmentioned excitement in enlisting. So, this availability only served to support or aid my addictive behaviors. I continued or in many ways even progressed in a lifestyle that involved alcohol and drug use on a daily basis. And, this now included a wide variety of drugs beyond just marijuana.

Drug use was not legal in the military; however, it certainly was widespread and a well-known problem after the war. Initially it was difficult to tell whether they merely turned their backs on it and ignored it or they just did not know how to control it. They were trying to get a handle on it and discourage it by incrementally "cracking down" on it in a variety of ways, yet they knew they could not just wage an all-out battle on users because of the overwhelming degree of the problem. A huge number of people would have been in jail or discharged. Most likely that would have left big gaps in the enlistment numbers and unfilled positions. They had been overlooking it for so long during that era because they no doubt had bigger issues to contend with during the war and they were now confronted with new young men and women coming into the military that were looking to experiment with drugs. That may not have been their primary reason for enlisting, but the recruits certainly were aware of the rumors surrounding the culture in the military and many were likely looking forward to it.

The attitude about drug use back then was almost the complete opposite of what it is today. There was a push to try and eradicate drug use in society as well as the military rather than legalize it like today's culture. If they only knew the truth about it. This book is not about drug use or abuse, so I do not want to give it too much attention here. But I do feel compelled to share these details and elaborate just a bit to help you understand the impact it had on my early life and set the path for many of the more "hard core" rehabilitative ministries that I would later serve in. Whether you realize it or not; alcohol and drug use impacts the church today by affecting the lives of both believers and non-believers alike.

The addictive properties of drugs and alcohol can also be a barricade that keeps people out of the church like it did with me and that is not a good thing! People with drug and alcohol problems who come to know Jesus face some hidden adversity with their testimonies and past lifestyles when they become known to others in the church. The church appears to love hearing about tantalizing testimonies, but people love gossip even more so. And, guess what… that ultimately causes church wounds for many individuals who sincerely yet unknowingly share their pasts. Do not be blinded to the fact that it does indeed happen in the church and most likely a lot more often than you think it does. My apologies for the sidebar here, but I do feel that it is important for me to point this out to those of you who think we do not cause church offenses intentionally. I can say without reservation that there is a lot of evidence showing the church's easily identifiable inability to view and forgive sin in the same unequivocal and unbiased way that God does, and it goes beyond my own observations or experiences.

Since the military was fervently trying to curb the widespread drug use during the 70's and 80's, it made it much harder to indulge in that type of lifestyle without being detected. And, with my ever-increasing involvement in the drug culture, I had to rely on an even higher level of sneakiness and covertness to keep from getting caught as well as avoid any criminal prosecution. Drug use turned into drug abuse and drug abuse evolved into dealing drugs. This required skills that went beyond my well-recognized ability to deceive and fool people on the surface. I knew that I would have to be one step ahead of the law all the time or smarter than them, for lack of a better way of putting it in order to avoid prosecution or getting caught. I am not sure that one can logically or grammatically say that "you can be good at a bad thing" ... however, if you can then I was pretty good at it. I had a lot of close calls but amazingly I was able to live a secret life largely undetected (and without criminal prosecution) for over four years in the military.

There are many individual stories and graphic details that I could share with you about those four years, but I am inclined to purposely use a refrained approach for several reasons. You may not recognize my approach as being "refrained" but trust me, it is. What I have written so far is purposeful and although some reading the book may not be able to relate to some of the details or stories; I am quite certain that many others will be able to. So, please bear with me. You also may not fully understand what some of this has to do with church offenses or a call to ministry, but each fragment is a piece of the puzzle that God put together or put back together in order to prepare me for ministry. A call that oftentimes caused me to wonder that perhaps my earlier lifestyle was more appealing in some ways than overcoming the many church offenses and the subsequent wounds that I would have to endure from the body of Christ. You would think that ministry and the church would be a much better environment than the worldly and resistant lifestyle but sometimes it just was not.

The world was admittedly carnal, but it was at least peaceful and arguably not as psychologically damaging. You see, you can look down upon those who are outside of the church as they lead a less than desirable or holy lifestyle if you like; but I can honestly tell you that many of them treat folks better than you could expect in some churches today. That is a shame. Now maybe you see why I have put these enlightening details into my book.

All that being said, and although I provide a lot of transparency in this book for the sake of accurately and honestly depicting my background; I am also driven to try and maintain my focus for this particular book. Though I believe that it is important for you to understand the journey leading up to my time in ministry; I do not want to have my personal testimony, or any salacious details unintentionally replace that focus with an emphasis on the life I came out of. Many people that know me or have heard a more complete or detailed personal testimony from me know that I have no qualms about honestly sharing more specific detail when it is appropriate or warranted.

I have learned over the years that there is a lot more to be lost or at stake than there is to be gained when someone offers too much information or specific details about their past. Even in the church. Anyone that gives a testimony will instantly become vulnerable to some degree. As I noted previously, I am tremendously aware of how powerful testimonies can be when people are able to relate to you; however, they can also be a devasting weapon against you when people develop wrong perspectives about you or even gossip about it. Please do not be fooled into thinking that it does not happen in the church, because I have seen it happen numerous times. Those instances represent some of the very church hurts that I am addressing in this book. A high level or general idea about one's past should be enough for grasping an understanding about their past and what their life was like when not serving God.

When it comes to testimonies another common and deceiving thought that many people in the church fall prey to is that the greater depths of sin that someone has been brought out of somehow makes a testimony more powerful. The fallacy in this is that the power of the testimony is not in what you have been saved from but rather in how you were saved from it. Although, heart wrenching stories can certainly help individuals that are in the same predicament...the testimony itself does not profit from the degree of just how bad the behavior was and thus should not be the emphasis of the testimony. The fact that God is able to bring you out of a lifestyle where all humanistic efforts have failed is where the power comes from. If you have trouble grasping these thoughts and concepts, then you may find yourself in the midst of causing a potential church offense in the future through your own mishandling or misinterpretation of someone's graphic and yet sober testimony.

My goal in this chapter was not to provide you with a tantalizing or entertaining story about my past that somehow captivates your interest. Even though I have shared a considerable amount for the purpose of transparency and to illustrate just how far I strayed from God during this period of my life; the main point was that I entered the military around the Vietnam era when the struggles with drug and alcohol abuse were at one of their highest levels and I easily embraced that lifestyle because of that environment and the circumstances in my life leading up to it. That I survived that time period absent of a more tragic outcome or any criminal prosecution for my activities is nothing short of a miracle. Many people have not been as fortunate as I was. For some reason, God provided unexplained grace for keeping me mostly unscathed through those years must surely have had my future in ministry in mind. I am sure that I did not survive merely because I was so good at escaping the perils of it all. But, what I am sure of is that I did not deserve His grace and mercy.

Additionally, a far more important meaning to grasp in this chapter is how all of this affected my spiritual life and the relationship with the church that was such a big part of my younger days. Had I drifted or strayed beyond a point of no return? Had everything that the church instilled in my early childhood years been undone? Although I was not living for God, I still believed in Him. I still considered myself "basically a good person" despite my life of self-indulgence and secular activity. Wasn't my otherwise good behavior and the resistance to cross some boundaries evidence that some Christian principles still existed somewhere within my character? Or was it conceivable that I was not even really a Christian any longer? Quite possibly some of you have wondered about these very same questions at some point in your own life.

I do not think that I ever attended a church service the entire time that I was in the military other than a few chapel services on the military base here and there. The services were called non-denominational or Protestant largely to differentiate them from the Catholic or Orthodox services, although they sure were not like the dynamic or charismatic services that I was accustomed to while growing up. They were very liturgical, dogmatic, and almost ceremonial. No powerful worship or preaching. The services seemed like something out of the 19th century rather than anything that could be classified as contemporary.

Essentially, the services amounted to a few old hymns with usually no accompanying music at all in most cases; some reciting of scripture and maybe a brief interpretation or message from the Chaplain. Some of that structure was no doubt due to the need for the military to try to satisfy "all" religions during their services. Subsequently, the services had very little impact on me other than to assert that I had at least attended church. Although, the services certainly didn't initiate any desire to return to the church right away or lead me to thinking that church was anything that I particularly needed at the time; I will say that something deep inside me still felt good for some reason and appeasing in the sense that I had at least attended a service.

Even though I did not feel immediately drawn back to the church during my time in the military, I remember that it was satisfying to think that I never totally lost where I came from. The few chapel services I attended helped to at least show me that I never "totally" lost my respect and love for the church. I often found myself defending its usefulness or impact on people's lives when scoffers or antagonists spoke ill of it. I still believed in treating others decently and respectfully. Particularly the elderly, disadvantaged or downtrodden. I still believed that God was real and active in our lives despite my worldly behavior and notwithstanding the church's boring religious services. I still believed that I needed God in my life, although only to the extent that it remained on my terms...like times of trouble when I felt that I "really" needed Him.

As my stint in the military was coming to an end; God placed my wife into my life. Not all marriages start out as the ideal Christian model or appear to be a wise move upfront and ours was no different in that regard. We dated for only a few months and most of that was long distance as I finished out my last year in the Navy. However, we did do our part in keeping the U.S. Postal Service and the phone companies in business. I spent probably close to $1/4^{th}$ of my monthly paycheck on long distance calls. We did not have cell phones back then so the pay phone booth in a local ferry terminal became like a second home to me. Although, it may have been a long-distance relationship, it was growing deep and in just a matter of months we were planning on getting married.

We did not have much money saved up and we did not really have solid plans laid out for the future, yet it did not seem to matter to us. The thought of marriage most likely looked like a disaster just waiting to happen to many people around us. In fact, many family members wanted us to wait a couple of years to get married as they expected us to fail. We just knew we loved each other, and my wife was willing to give up everything back home and follow me anywhere. It is hard to imagine that God would have endorsed it either or much less considered it part of the long-term plan. However, it is much easier to look back nearly forty years later and see all the reasons that God purposely brought her into my life and the timing in doing so. I am sure it saved me from being on the brink of disastrous consequences in my life.

My wife was young, very pretty and had the most wonderful smile in the world. She still has that beautiful smile! There was indeed a physical attraction and I knew that I loved her, yet I would discover many more things about her that helped to make up the glue for holding our marriage and household together for so many years. Her strength, courage, love of family, determination, insight, patience, and amazing instincts have shown her to be an enviable example of a wife, mother, and grandmother. I could have never foreseen all the precious commodities that were hidden inside of her. Yes, her outer beauty initially attracted me but there was also something deeper spiritually at work, and neither one of us were aware of it nor would have probably understood it at the time.

We have oftentimes told people in our marriage classes that we are likely not a great example to follow. At least regarding planning, spiritual condition, finances, or career planning anyway. On the surface our marriage may look like it had the ideal beginning since we have been married for nearly forty years at the writing of this book; but, our initial approach and timing were not what would likely be regarded as a recipe for success in most instances. With that acknowledgement in mind, however; it is a great example of what God can do despite your disposition or shortcomings when He chooses to bless you and has a plan for your life. Apparently, circumstances and the fact that a lot of change still needs to take place in your life is of no consequence to God when He knows and is planning your future.

They say "you can't change someone" just by marrying them and although there is much truth in that because they must want to change themselves; you can certainly be the motivation or inspiration in their life to change. Especially if you truly love them and you love God like my wife does. I would discover years later that it was my wife's love for God and her willingness to trust Him in everything that made her so special. She would prove to be that motivation and inspiration in my life that would open the door for change and ultimately bring me back to the church as well as a life of ministry.

Special Note*****
This chapter was indeed a difficult one to write. I prayed and struggled with the idea of just how much do I need to share about my past? How detailed do I get? If my goal is to ultimately address how offenses are hurting the church, then how relevant is it to reveal my past personal experiences prior to entering ministry? Do they really need to know about my upbringing? Would it be the least bit helpful or complement the book? And, what about those who might initially think that it is too much personal information for their liking? Will I lose credibility with those inside the church that might allow some negative perceptions about my past life to get in the way of accepting what I have to say despite how factual it may be?

Because I believe that what we learn in our early life is extremely important and that it will have an impact on how we deal with life's problems later on; I concluded that it is indeed important for me to lay some groundwork on my early life's experiences. Especially since the church was a critical element in my early childhood development and many of my life experiences negatively impacted that. It would also afford the opportunity to connect with many people outside of the church that have similar experiences and wonder if God can ever use them in ministry. And a lot of what I went through or experienced in the secular environment would prove to be useful and relevant when it came to understanding and overcoming church offenses many years later.

As I prayerfully considered this chapter over a long period of time (and I'm talking years here); God helped to remind me that there will still undoubtedly be some who read this book and need to feel that connection in the beginning in order to open a door of opportunity that changes their life. A connection with someone who does not mirror the church poster child or a career Christian that they may be accustomed to encountering or hearing from. One who clearly knows what is like to not come from a "perfect" Christian household. One who had to survive in this world without much of the support and structure that many Christian families get to enjoy.

And yet, I still know that including some of the details about my early life which depicts an ungodly lifestyle comes at the risk that some people in the Church community might question my motivations or ministerial credibility. There are some people within the church who also struggle with colorful or eye-opening testimonies of others because they have never had to personally deal with severe issues like dysfunctional families, divorce, homelessness, abuse, alcoholism, or drugs. That is not their fault and they should feel blessed for having escaped all those things. However, it is a challenge for them to fully understand the importance in connecting with others going through those life situations. A bit of irony is that the church oftentimes seems to embrace or rejoice for those kinds of testimonies, yet their level of joy is seemingly enhanced because they perceive the sin of the one giving a testimony to be so much greater than their own. That is religion; not relationship my friends!

I do want to say one last thing about testimonies and help you to understand something critical about them. Do not envy nor disdain the testimony of others. The glory is in how God brings people out of lifestyles where the world fails to. The glory is not in the depth of depravity they are involved with. Sin is sin and you should count your blessings anytime you do not have to endure or go through what someone else has. Developing this simple but clear understanding and sincere appreciation about testimonies will help you to avoid causing a church offense because of a failure on your part to view or handle them as God does.

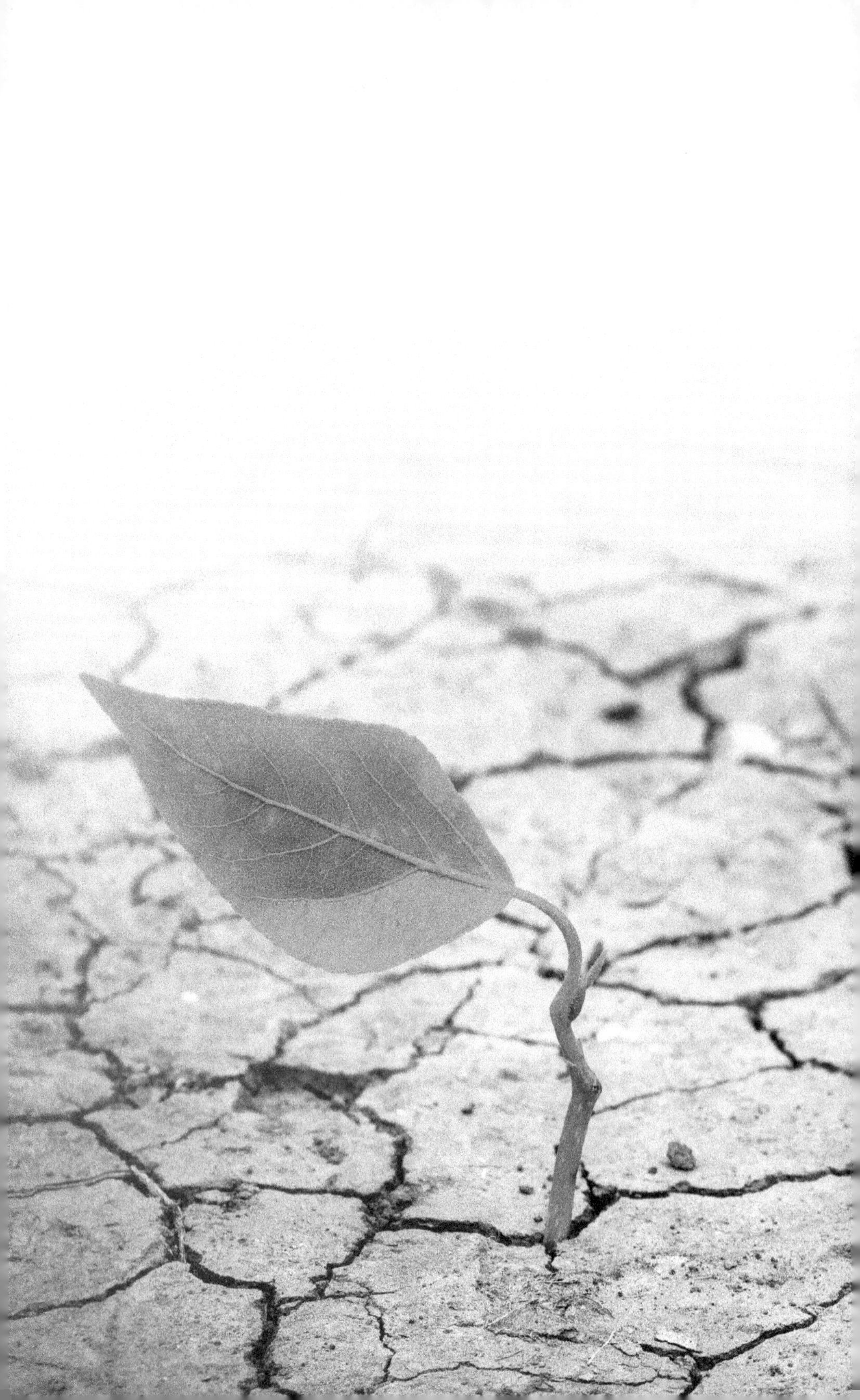

4

CALL TO MINISTRY

After getting married, my wife joined me up in Washington where I was stationed. As my enlistment in the military was coming to an end, I really had no idea that I would eventually enter into a life of ministry. And, if my lifestyle at that time was any kind of an indicator it would not have seemed likely to many other people either. I was in my young 20's and still largely involved with worldly behavior. Although I must say that meeting my wife was helping to temper my activity and she slowly started to inspire me to change because she was not involved with the same partying lifestyle that I was. I still indulged in a lot of those behaviors. Many of them secretly, but I was slowly moving away from a lot of my old carnal behaviors.

We did not regularly set foot inside of a church yet, outside of an occasional wedding or funeral. I am sure that we both probably would have insisted that we considered ourselves Christians because of our mutual beliefs and values. Many people, including most of our family members and friends, did not attend church either and yet they still professed to be Christian. A growing and popular interpretation being adopted by many was that being a Christian largely depended on just believing in God and not so much on your behavior or lifestyle. Unless it was so outrageous and bad that most people could logically assume that you could not possibly be a Christian. Such as severely criminal or highly immoral behavior.

The culture in America was starting to develop a negative if not even inflammatory perspective on regular church goers with names like Jesus freaks, Holy Rollers and Bible thumpers. Those inside the church were oftentimes described as pious, self-righteous, holier-than-thou, or even weak minded. Many people outside of the church laughingly or jokingly referred to themselves as heathens or their lifestyle as heathen behavior poking fun at the idea that anyone who did not regularly attend church must be a non-believer. A growing population seemed to be embracing the idea that their lack or even absence of attendance had little or nothing to do with their Christian walk. For others it just was not a priority in their life. In other words, church attendance was slowly starting to be regarded as an unimportant or unnecessary component for defining what it was to be a Christian. Unless you happened to be super religious or felt morally superior to others.

My wife and I most likely fell into the category of those who did not think of it as a priority in their life. We did not despise or hate the church. We just did not see it as critical or essential. We both believed in God and much of our lives were structured around the biblical principles we grew up around, so we were not bad people or treated others badly. And, we were not staying away from church because of any serious church offenses. I do not think we had really encountered or at least were aware of any up to that point. Though I must admit that it is rather difficult to encounter them if you are not going to church very often! We did not take much time to consider how key attending church could be to the lifestyle that we lived or how it impacted our spiritual growth. Real spiritual growth was a foreign or vague concept to us at that time.

One of the best decisions we made during the early part of our marriage was waiting for five years to have any children. It was more because of our own self-centered needs than because of any wise decision-making on our part, but nonetheless it was a good early path to take. Our aspirations and our lifestyles were not necessarily ideal for raising a family and it would have undoubtedly only made things worse or even more difficult. Though that concern does not seem to impact many young people's decisions today when they get pregnant right away or are getting married because they are pregnant. We were acutely aware of our financial disposition and struggles in the early going. The first few years of marriage were just as tough as most people proclaim them to be. Especially financially and that has the tendency to carry over into other important areas like your relationship and how you treat one another.

When I was discharged from the Navy in 1981 after completing my enlistment; it was one of the roughest economical times for the entire country. Many of you probably are not aware of how difficult of a time period it was. There simply were no decent jobs to be found. Even part time or low paying jobs were scarce and taken up by unemployed people with stronger work histories. I always thought that being in the military would give me an advantage, but unfortunately the economy was so much in the tank that my military experience was almost meaningless. We were still living in Washington state and it was an even more dire situation as the Naval Shipyards and Boeing had just recently laid off thousands of people.

It got so bad economically for us at the time that my wife took a fast food job at Burger King. To a large degree it was just so we had something to eat for free and not because it had lucrative potential in any particular way. I think that I had enough Whoppers back then to last me for a lifetime. It was nearly impossible for me to find full-time work, so I ended up taking one of the hardest possible jobs on earth by Selling Kirby vacuum cleaners. Selling is somewhat of a misnomer though because it was a rarity to actually sell one. They were expensive to begin with and the horrible economy did not help matters. Since it was solely based on commission, you only got paid when you sold one. I think I only sold one in the few months I tried to make a go of it, and the people who bought it ended up returning it within a few days, so I really did not make any money for even the one. Nonetheless, I can always claim that it was another one of the many interesting jobs that I have had in my life. And, strangely enough it gave me an evangelistic opportunity many years later when I met someone who also had tried to sell them, and I was able to lead them to the Lord because of that connection. It is commonly said that "God works in strange or mysterious ways." Some of you probably have no idea just how strange that is!

We slowly had to sell off most of our belongings and ended up moving into a small dilapidated apartment. We had little furniture left other than a small kitchen table with two chairs. We did not even have a bed, just a mattress on the floor. We probably should have headed home earlier however we were stubborn and determined to make it on our own. The thought of returning home penniless and jobless would be an embarrassing or shameful reminder of everyone's advice to wait on marriage.

Despite our declining and deteriorating lifestyle, my wife never blamed me for our situation and was always encouraging or thinking positive. She shrugged off most of the inconveniences and lack of possessions. As we look back we both know it was one of the most difficult times in our life, however it was also amazing to us how you could still enjoy life and each other without any money or the material things that so often define a good living. Spending time together and limiting our ventures to those things you could do free (like walks, visits to the ocean or parks, etc.) was seemingly enough for us because we truly loved each other and just being together was seemingly good enough. Though life did appear to be simpler sometimes without the obligations and temptations that having money can bring; the reality of our rapidly declining situation would eventually catch up with us. You still need a job and money to pay rent, buy food, purchase gas, and pay the other bills that you just cannot escape.

Ultimately, we were forced to move back home to Nebraska. We were broke, discouraged, and unable to find any kind of decent work for months while we were in Washington. I dreaded moving back home as it was disheartening, and we would metaphorically be returning "with our tails between our legs." Everyone thought we had gotten married too soon anyway and that we would not be able to make it on our own, so it opened the opportunities for receiving a big "I told you so."

Although, I was twenty-one when we got married; my wife was just eighteen and many people thought we were too young and unprepared. Especially our families. Some of their speculation no doubt had to do with my worldly and bad boy lifestyle back then and some of it because I probably didn't seem like the ideal candidate or someone as having the potential to adequately support and take care of a family. What made it even more difficult to have to move back home was the fact that we really had no choice other than to stay with family for a short period of time until we could find work and get back on our feet. It was more humiliating than it was humbling.

Fortunately, I was able to find work right away. Amazingly it was the very next day after we returned home. That was extremely favorable and a blessing for me as I had been out of work for several months already and if I didn't find work quickly, I knew that the wisdom in waiting to get married would likely only be exploited further. It took us awhile to save up enough money to move out on our own and it was a very tense and trying time during that period. Anyone that has had to move in with family as a young adult probably understands what I mean by that. To our good fortune (and blessing), my wife found a job in short time as well. Eventually we were able to establish somewhat of a stable life, save some money and move out on our own once again. From that point on things have always seemed to get just a little bit better for us. Certainly, we never have been able to avoid all rough times or adversity, though every challenge has brought on a new opportunity that seems to build on the last one and exceed the provisions of the prior experience. In hindsight, it seems God has always kept His promises and given us just what we need or beyond.

Although I had many different jobs during the next couple of decades, I was never out of work for very long. Partly because we both had strong work ethics and partly because a great many job changes were either promotions or moving in the right direction. We both always felt the need if not the obligation to work or immediately find work. And, aside from our own work ethic it also seemed that God always found ways to bless us. Even during those times where we were not necessarily living for God.

My wife's work history was far less revolving or complicated than mine was. She landed a job at the time with a company that was considered one of the best to work for in Omaha. She stayed and moved up in that company for decades while I still tried to figure out what it was that I wanted to do in life. Or, what I was called to do. Although, a "calling" for ministry still had not crossed my mind just yet. My wife was technically the bread winner during that time with a secure and increasingly well-paying position. In the meantime, I held a lot of different positions with different companies. Although I stayed employed and each new position surpassed the compensation or benefits of the old one, it seemed that I was still behind her in being the main provider for our family. That was tough because that time period was still under the mindset of the previous generation that the man should be the main if not sole provider of the household. Even many churches saw it that way. Although I had a consistent and growing income for years; none of the jobs probably would be thought of as prestigious. However, God opened an opportunity for me at a company with a union contract that finally allowed me to make a substantial or impressive wage. I finally surpassed my wife in earnings, and I was no longer under the shadow of being thought of as a poor provider. We finally reached a point where we could seriously consider having a family and even buy a house.

It was not until around five years after being married that we finally started making our way back to the church. We had built a new house in the small community that my wife grew up in and it seemed like we were on our way to realizing the American dream. We had two children right after one another (a boy and a girl), a golden retriever and even a minivan. Our kids were starting to get more involved in neighborhood or pre-school activities and it seemed like we were doing everything young families are supposed to do.

My wife was the first one to be drawn back to the church. She appeared to be drawn back through the ongoing communication with her sister about her sister's newfound interest in church and spirituality. However, I believe that my wife was also motivated on her own when our lives and priorities began to change with the start of a family. After buying a new house and somewhat altering our lifestyle to a more family focused approach; my wife felt the urge to start looking for a local church to attend. She had mentioned it to me already on several occasions. Without a doubt she had developed her own yearning and desire to know God more closely. I believe that it has probably always existed in her. Regardless of whether her sister initiated the spark, or she uncovered the desire on her own; the point is that it was indeed happening.

Eventually my wife found a local Baptist church that was close to where we lived, and she started to visit it. She had grown up Baptist and we were married in her Baptist church, so it seemed like a logical or natural path for her to choose. She would take our two young children with her and she gladly attended even if it meant going without me. I did not accompany them at first as I did not see the personal need for it and always had some convenient excuse. Nevertheless, it did not stop her from going. To her credit she did not get angry with me or make it an issue that I was not attending with them. She was determined to do it regardless of my willingness to join. Although she always graciously and excitedly invited me. I just was not really interested in attending church yet. I am not exactly sure why I was not interested considering my upbringing or church background, but apparently I had grown apart from it and it was just not a high priority in my life.

Over time my wife was able to persuade me to visit with them. I did not really go with them out of any kind of compelling feeling or of my own initial desire to attend. It was probably more to appease her than out of my own interest or drive. I do not mean appeasing her in a way that sounds like giving in or to simply stop her from inviting me; but rather just wanting to make her happy. I have always wanted to make her happy just out of my love for her and because she was my best friend. Perhaps, in a way I also felt that I was just doing what most good families and husbands were supposed to do. I have always been driven towards being a good husband because of growing up in an atmosphere where marriage and divorce were so easily taken for granted or with such little regard for its implications. In other words, I did not want to be like my parents. Unknowingly at the time, that is when things really started to change in our lives. It was the beginning of a spiritual change that causes or motivates you to take an inventory of your life and move towards changes in all those areas that need it.

I have told people over the years that my kids were the biggest inspiration for me to quit drugs altogether, and they were. I had tremendously pared down my use over the years for the sake of my wife, however I was still using them occasionally and was at the minimum still a social partier. Something inside of me was starting to change and I knew that I desired more for my kids. I knew it affected the quality of the time I gave them, and I also did not want them growing up with the same challenges or roadblocks that I had. Initially, I do not think I looked at my shift in thinking as having any spiritual significance or origin. It was the early stages of conviction and drawing us back to the church, so I consciously and conveniently attributed the changes in my life more to my own personal convictions or self-analysis. In other words, I felt that it was because "I" thought that it was the right thing to do. Not because God thought it was.

Initially it was a bit of a challenge for me to attend church because of it being a Baptist church. I was mainly used to Pentecostal churches or more charismatic services, so I cannot tell you how boring it seemed to me at first. I even silently in my head made fun of their reserved worship styles, their emphasis or love for old hymns and preaching that was not as dynamic as what I grew up with. On the other hand, I kind of liked that it was actually a safe place for me to start because I could go without having to outwardly be excited or demonstrative like the Pentecostal or spirit-filled churches that I grew up in. And, I was not pressured to be immediately involved or engaged like you normally would be encouraged to do in some of the more charismatic or Pentecostal churches. Yet, even though I enjoyed just being another body in the services; something was happening inside of me that was slowly starting to take effect. I cannot say that I was totally aware of what it was at the time... but I knew something was happening and inspiring me to change my life in many practical ways.

I did not mind going to church with my family and you might even say that I was starting to enjoy it a little bit. The people were nice, it was good for my kids and family and even causing me to start changing things in my life. But I can tell you that I was not "all in" just yet. Then things took a dramatic turn for me. My sister-in-law was always talking to my wife about church and the Holy Spirit. My wife was growing spiritually at a rapid pace and getting hungrier for God. She was loving the impact it was having on her family. So, my sister-in-law decided to send me a book. Maybe to help accelerate my progress or ignite the same level of fire that they were experiencing. She sent a book called *The Invisible World* by well-known pastor and author Greg Laurie. The book takes a very practical approach in helping people to understand how the supernatural and spiritual world works. I was not into daily Bible reading or devotionals just yet, but I did like reading and had read several other spiritual books that had been given to me. My wife and her sister always seemed to be looking for ways to get me to go deeper or match their level of excitement. Although many of the books I had read were helpful up to this point; none of them would impact me as much as this one would.

I am not exactly sure why, but I finally picked up the book and started reading it one evening when my wife and kids had gone to bed. I cannot say why I chose that particular evening or if I were drawn to it purposely at that exact time, but I do remember that I could not put it down. I read the whole book in one sitting. Pastor Laurie provides a story in the book about two neighbors. The story creatively if not covertly turns out to illustrate the gospel message in a very practical sense. The message was so powerful that it caused me to have a spiritual encounter right then. I got on my knees in my own living room as the sun was rising and prayed for God to become more real in my life. I had prayed a prayer of salvation years before, but this was different. This was an issue of needing a spiritual awakening and God's power in my life. I certainly had not anticipated this moment earlier in the evening when I first started reading the book and I was overwhelmed with the realness of God's actual presence in my living room. I did not need a church, worship music playing in the background or a plea from the pulpit. Just me and God. Pastor Laurie is still not even aware of the impact or significance that his book had in my life.

Perhaps, someday I will have the opportunity to share it with him. Though I am sure he is probably aware by now that many lives have been impacted by his book over the years.

From that time on our lives changed rapidly. We started attending church regularly and we were both starting to spiritually grow at an accelerated pace. We started to get more connected with others in the church and involved in church activities. Both of us started to incorporate new disciplines in our lives like daily Bible reading, memorizing scripture and joining a small Bible study group. The pastor was a huge part of the growth we were experiencing who took a special interest in us and also started mentoring me. He became a great friend over the years and one that I will always be extremely grateful for because of his investment in me. He convinced me to enroll and participate weekly in credited discipleship and Bible courses that the Baptist churches offered. A hunger and fire in my soul was developing that inspired me to study nearly everything in my path. I studied the Bible, commentaries, church history, denominations, theology, leadership, cults, and evangelism.

**Even though I did not fully recognize it yet;
he was orchestrating an extremely fast paced discipleship
program that would set us on a path towards ministry.**

Ultimately, we took on our first role in ministry as the youth leaders of the Baptist church that we were attending. It was a role that we held and grew in for several years. Yet, it still was not enough for my wife. It was not because the position was unfulfilling. We really enjoyed the youth and learned a tremendous amount about serving in ministry. She just wanted more.

Her hunger and thirst were growing out of a desire to know more about the Holy Spirit and living a "spirit-led or spirit-filled" life.

The Baptist church recognized the Holy Spirit and the importance of the active role of the Holy Spirit in the life of the believer. However, the denomination was typically more reserved in theologically defining the "presence" or "gifts" of the Holy Spirit than the more charismatic churches. There was a movement in many of the churches towards establishing a freer worship style and balancing between traditional hymns and a contemporary praise and worship, but it oftentimes met some resistance or at least the drawing of some boundaries. Many Baptist churches tried to encourage people that it was okay to clap or raise your hands, however the number of people comfortable in doing so were few, and the level of awkwardness or embarrassment of others seeing you do it was visibly apparent. Manifestations such as speaking in tongues, prophecy, anointing, or healing were still mostly taboo if not frowned upon.

I must give my pastor friend from this church credit for having the courage to support the move to a freer style of worship and even being open to a more spirit-filled environment. It was no doubt extremely difficult to try and balance between the populations of those who were more traditionalists and others wanting the church to be open to that freedom. He did a wonderful job of understanding and embracing both populations despite the vulnerability it posed for him. He faced opposition from board members, their wives and prominent leaders or substantial "givers" in the body. He was a good friend and so I knew that the strife and division within the church was taking their toll on him. It was probably our first glimpse of church offenses from a leader's perspective and a glaring look at the behind the scenes struggles within church administration or government. We were just beginning to learn how religion and theology can cause devasting consequences and offenses to a church and many of its people in leadership. It is not a pretty picture of Christian character or behavior to behold.

The struggle in the Baptist church (and other denominations as well) over worship styles and theological positions would continue into the 21st century. Although the struggles have not come without pain or disastrous outcomes in some instances; I am glad that many of these churches have survived and now enjoy a bit more freedom in their worship styles and more openness in their theological positions regarding the Holy Spirit's role. Certainly not because Pentecostals or charismatic believers have it all nailed down correctly; but because our freedom in worship and doctrines should not be bound by religious dogmas and ideology that does not align with biblical teaching or is arguably based on preference. Unfortunately, that church underwent a church split sometime after we had left due to the division and disagreement amongst them. That is especially saddening because of our personal attachment to the church and because there were so many great people that we knew. I feel deeply for them regardless of what specific doctrinal position they may have supported or how they felt about the changes happening in the church. We did not leave this church because of the ongoing strife. We actually left before things ever got out of control. Much of it was not always visibly apparent and had not yet reached the level of an imminent split. We would eventually leave because it was time to continue with our journey in ministry. Nonetheless, we were still a witness to what religion can quickly do to a church.

Meanwhile as we were still attending and serving at the Baptist church, my wife's hunger, and curiosity in wanting to know more about the Holy Spirit was increasing. So, we started secretly visiting a local Pentecostal church while we were still leading the youth at our Baptist church. This was actually a good thing because we were able to go back and impart a lot of the growth we were experiencing into our youth at the Baptist church. Our pastor supported us visiting the Pentecostal church for personal spiritual hunger reasons and he was convinced that God had put it on our hearts for a specific purpose. Some people in the congregation immediately questioned whether it was good for us to still lead the youth under these circumstances. They were fearful and concerned about what the impact of any spirit filled, or spirit led emphasis would have on their young people. Ironically, many of the concerned parents, their grown children and their families are in spirit-filled churches today! We never abused our privileges or circumvented any parent's wishes; we just introduced them to a freer worship and did not shy away from talking about the importance of the Holy Spirit while keeping it all in biblical context. We left them with probably one of the most "on fire" Baptist youth groups in the city at the time despite its smaller size.

During our intermittent but increasing visits, my wife was developing a love for the worship and the newfound emphasis on the presence or anointing of the Holy Spirit. I grew up in that atmosphere, so it was not entirely all that new to me, but it was fresh for her and it did start to bring back much of the hunger and love for the church I used to have. In fairness; even though I grew up in Pentecostal churches I did not have a real deep personal knowledge or understanding of what it meant to be Holy Spirit filled. I knew about speaking in tongues and prophecy but did not fully or deeply understand all of that yet from a spiritual standpoint. I did know that something caused a dramatic change in people's lives creating a visible level of excitement, joy and passion about Jesus that just did not seem as evident in traditional environments not emphasizing a spirit-filled life. I am not going to get into all the arguments about being filled with the Holy Spirit, the infilling of the Holy Spirit or answering the question, "isn't everyone filled with the Holy Spirit when they are saved." That is another topic that goes well beyond the scope of this book. I am just telling you that there is a visible difference between when you choose to emphasize and embrace the role or presence of the Holy Spirit as opposed to when you do not.

Eventually, we knew it became time for us to move on and explore the path that God was leading us to. With the blessing from our pastor we finally made a change. It was bittersweet because you hate to leave behind those who you have built a special relationship with (especially the youth in this case) yet the excitement surrounding the unknown potential is compelling. Part of the decision-making for initiating the change was that we knew it would provide a variety of new ministry opportunities and the chance to go to an accredited Bible school. My wife believed that I had a calling on my life and she was in full support of that. So, I started the program that ultimately led to me becoming a licensed minister. I grew to learn even more about the Bible, God, and the Holy Spirit than I had ever imagined was possible in such a short amount of time. Yes, I grew up in a Pentecostal environment and even made a commitment to Christ in my early years but there was so much more to learn and experience. In all honesty, despite that I had been exposed to countless spirit-filled services and the teachings associated with the Holy Spirit; I did not fully comprehend the role or gifts of the Holy Spirit back in my early years as much as I was starting to now. Let alone what it truly meant to be filled with the Holy Spirit.

While completing my Bible schooling, we volunteered for a variety of ministries as we got more and more connected (or plugged in as they like to say). Our primary ministry was in working with the youth once again. However, we became even more engaged with those outside of the church than we had previously. We did things that many called "radical" back then like outreaches, street evangelism and reaching out to the homeless or less fortunate. We had developed a heart that was soft towards those that were lost, in bondage or in need. I guess they called it radical because those ministries cause you to get out of your comfort zones, go outside the church walls and actually do something rather than just sit inside the confines of the church building and merely talk about or acknowledge the existence of an unbelieving population. Radical ministry allowed the opportunity to face the many societal and spiritual issues that existed outside the walls of the church and were in need of the gospel message. I can tell you without reservation that evangelizing or witnessing to those outside the church walls is typically not the number one preference for serving the church. Even in those that list themselves as evangelical churches. Especially, if it involves ministering to the homeless or downtrodden. Those ministries may well be the toughest ones to be involved with. I say that not because of the difficulty in serving in them, but because during our years of ministry in those areas we learned what a perpetual problem it was for us to recruit people in the church to join us in those activities. Or, to keep them interested and committed in that area for any length of time. So, in that respect I guess it is "radical." But we loved it!

In addition to serving in those ministries and while I was finishing my Bible schooling, my wife became involved with the worship team. This was quite a bit different than the worship at the Baptist church and she absolutely enjoyed it. She has always loved singing, praising and worshiping God and this gave her an opportunity to be freer in her worship than ever before. This church had some of the most dynamic and powerful worship that we have been associated with over the years. Not that other worship teams in other churches have not been good. They just were special. It went well beyond just being talented musicians or singers. They really knew how to worship. As my wife would say, "they really knew how to usher in the Holy Spirit." The church had a lively if not rocking choir that my wife was a part of. It was not unusual to be worn out spiritually and physically after worship was over. Yet, at the same time you would feel revitalized. If people earnestly wanted to know how to define or describe what you mean by spirit-filled; all you would have to do is attend one of those services with the genuine desire to want more of God, sincerely set aside your hindrances or inhibitions and you would understandably know or experience what I am talking about. It is a real experience between you and God on your own that goes beyond what anyone could fabricate or incite merely because they can play or sing good.

It took several years to complete my Bible schooling and obtain my license to minister. By then my calling as an evangelist was starting to become more apparent. I intensely studied all the great evangelists that I could. I looked at both contemporary and past evangelists. I researched their techniques, their stories, and their passion. I read through the Bible more times than I can remember. I was becoming so familiar with the scriptures that it became a part of me. It was more than memorizing the verses but rather seeking to know them spiritually and having them deeply embedded in my heart or soul like David described having hidden in his heart. I had this inexplicable deep burning within my heart and soul to share and defend the gospel. It was not entirely a strange feeling considering the denomination that I was associated was known for its evangelical mission, however this felt different than just volunteering to serve in the church or even being called into ministry in general. Was I specifically being called to be a pastor or an evangelist? I was not sure, yet.

Some people reading this book may ask "aren't all pastors or even all people in the church called to be an evangelist in some way?" Yes, in a way. However, having a deep appreciation for evangelism is different than actually being called to be an evangelist. The denomination I come from makes a distinction between those called to be pastors and those called to be evangelists. And, the Bible does as well. Despite all my training and knowledge about the different "offices" of the church, it was still difficult for me to sort out whether I had the calling of being a pastor or that of an evangelist. Practically, all of my friends in ministry and leaders in the church affirmed at one time or another that I was undoubtedly called to be an evangelist. Yet, I still entertained the idea that I was also called to be a pastor.

Part of the confusion may have come from knowing that my grandmother had prophesied over me decades earlier about becoming a pastor and an evangelist. I did not fully comprehend the significance of that back then, as I was very young and was only reminded of it by her years later. I did not really understand prophecy or even put much weight to it at that early age. And, I certainly did not comprehend the difference in the calling between a pastor and an evangelist back then either. However, now that a life of ministry was starting to become a reality, I tried to figure out what her prophecy meant that I had been told about. I knew that I liked to preach and defend the Holy Word like an evangelist. I knew that my skills were developing in this area as I studied evangelism and the evangelists. I knew that there is an art to it (the art of persuasion) despite that it is still the Holy Spirit doing the work, so I worked hard at creative ways to share the gospel. What I did not know or completely understand was what I was being specifically called to do by God.

I knew my heart was telling me that I was called to be an evangelist, but my mind was telling me that I may be called to be a pastor instead. Not that a pastor cannot be an evangelist at times, or an evangelist cannot be a pastor in many ways. But they can be different roles or callings. An evangelist might never obtain the title of pastor and a pastor may ever fully immerse themselves in the functions of an evangelist. Likewise, an evangelist could also be asked to fill the "role" of a pastor assignment and a pastor may also take on the role of an evangelist in some instances.

Why is it so important to know the difference? Because when you do not fully understand the difference in the specific calling, it can lead to seeking a title or position instead of seeking what role God has planned for you. As I look back on things many years later; I believe much of the confusion for me was because that I selfishly wanted the title of pastor, but embraced the calling of an evangelist. I just did not realize it at the time. The lack of understanding this at the beginning would eventually cause problems for me later in ministry.

You have heard me say evangelist and evangelism several times now and maybe you feel that you have some idea of what I am referring to. Perhaps you do. But I am quite sure that many people if asked would be just as confused as I was about the differing calls in ministry between a pastor and evangelist. Some in the Church may not even really understand what an evangelist is or does. Many people that I have met or talked to in the church think of it as someone who just reaches out to the lost and shares the gospel. Someone who maybe shows up occasionally to hold revivals or crusades. Some even relish the idea that God has given the church some special gift or person like an evangelist. They errantly think that an evangelist is a substitute for those in the general congregation who might be too afraid or feel ill-equipped to share the gospel. But, I can tell you that being an evangelist is so much more than that. And, so is their responsibility and accountability to God.

I believe an evangelist is a little bit of a pastor, a little bit of a teacher, a little bit of a prophet, a little bit of an overseer and a whole lot of being a preacher. Even when not "officially" preaching at the time. Their heart aches for the lost, it burns for God and it breaks for the church when it is not doing what it should be doing. They seek and hope for wisdom as well as God's will in the church versus popularity or comfort. They are quiet a lot more often than you might think, but are outspoken when called to be. They are always watching or listening. They are not afraid to speak the truth despite the consequences, but they look to try and do so only under the anointing of the Holy Spirit. Contrary to popular belief, most of them prefer to spend more time praying quietly, where they can hear and talk with God in private, more so than they bravely do in public. When called to be an evangelist, they are much like Jonah, Jeremiah, or Paul where it is a calling that God will not allow you to escape no matter how hard you try or desire. It is embedded in your soul. They seem to psychologically drift somewhere between soberly accepting their own lack of righteousness which comes only from God, and pride which is oftentimes their undoing.

I do not believe that the calling can really be fully understood or all that easily explained to someone who at some point has not had that burden. It may be something you could pray for or seek but it is not something you merely fabricate or attain on your own. All of the evangelists that I know of did not ask for it and often wondered why God picked them. However, if you do seek it then be aware that it is not something you can easily or readily give back to God. The Lord knows that I have tried to escape the burden of an evangelist many times in my life. And to be honest...there are times where I still want to give it back to God. I am hoping that the above description will help you to not only better comprehend the heart and makeup of evangelists, but also provide a clearer understanding of the context and content of my books.

5

THE EARLY CHALLENGES IN MINISTRY

After I finished my Bible schooling and officially became a licensed minister, I felt like I was ready to enter into some kind of ministry, but I had no idea what door would open. My wife and I were open to accepting a position at a church or some ministry outside of the church; however, we wanted to be patient and make sure we were being led by God and that we were doing so in His timing. We did not feel any sense of urgency because we loved the church we were at and certainly had plenty of opportunities to minister and volunteer there. We had already spent many years at this church learning and growing while I completed school. The time we spent there also afforded us the opportunity to learn all about serving in various functional areas of the church including church administration and the "business" side of the church. These were great years in ministry as volunteers that helped us to learn invaluable lessons that would stay with us throughout all our years and in our times of ministry. No job was too small, humbling, or menial when it comes to learning how to serve. And yes, that includes cleaning toilets. During this time, we were fortunate to be shielded from church offenses because of the great leadership at the church. I am sure the church had their fair share of them, but the leadership did such a great job of quickly resolving them that they never seemed to evolve into major issues or be noticeably out front.

Despite getting my license and feeling like I was ready for full-time ministry, my wife and I were willing to wait upon God to point us in the right direction. So, we just continued to serve in the capacities that we had been serving in. I already had numerous opportunities to preach and develop my skills in that area as well as in evangelism, so I felt like I was equipped and ready to take on the task of being a preacher. Yes, it is true that it does require some development of those skills. If you look at some of the prophets (e.g. Elijah and Elisha) you can realize that no one is born with them or at least from a refined and polished perspective.

Oftentimes, you need to wait in the wings while God develops you, prepares you for ministry or gets you "up to speed." If you doubt that, then just ask someone how they felt after their first opportunity to speak in front of a crowd. Or, refer to your own feelings after a job interview and reflect on how you felt afterwards knowing that you could have perhaps presented yourself more articulately than you actually did. Experience is a valuable learning tool. Especially when you are talking about people's lives and souls. Despite my feeling of readiness, it did not happen right away. For the longest period of time (or so it seemed like forever), we were challenged with being content with where God had us serving at the time. It would take over a year before any opportunity at all opened for me.

Disappointingly, my first assignment or opportunity was in children's ministry in the church we were still attending and serving in. It would involve serving under one of the few female pastors in this particular denomination at the time. Part of the denomination's doctrine was the belief that men were not intended to serve "under" women. Women definitely could serve in the church but not necessarily as pastors and specifically not over men. Over time this had changed to allowing them to serve in pastoral or leadership roles if it was not a senior pastor position and more specifically if it was directly related to children's or women's ministries. Ironically, today that denominations perspective has changed or opened up even more to allow women to serve as leaders or pastors beyond those roles.

I find it amazing how theological or biblical stances all of a sudden change over the years, don't you? The Bible does not change, but man is somehow forced to revisit their earlier doctrinal positions on Church protocol or standard practice. Does that mean that God has somehow changed His mind over time? Or, does it mean that man is simply forced to evaluate their past errors in properly applying His Word? Perhaps, they are merely succumbing to cultural pressure? These are a few profound questions for church leaders to consider and answer to!

In complete honesty, I was initially disappointed in my first ministry opportunity outside of what we had been previously volunteering for. Partially, because I had been indoctrinated to believe that men should not have to serve under women in the church (so far as positions go) and partly because it was not representative of the great opportunities that I thought I would have once I obtained my license. It seemed like a slap in the face or a wake-up call for me to the realities of how many people obtain if not inherit church positions. I am just being honest with you. I was not directly related to anyone in the church, so I entertained the thought that perhaps that was the reason I was not immediately elevated to a "higher" position. It always seemed like pastor's and leaders' kids were recognized as having a call on their life and somehow more easily got a position. So, perhaps that was another challenge I would have to overcome. Or, was there another reason why I needed to serve in this area?

Although, it was certainly humbling (and disappointing), in many ways this first assignment would prove to be critical in teaching me how to really serve. Ultimately, this opportunity would prove to be one of the best assignments and learning experiences I ever had. I had an opportunity to grow and learn so much under this great lady who loved God, loved others, and exhaustingly worked to bless others. Serving under her helped me to immediately learn about humility and I had no idea how valuable that would prove to be down the road. Especially when it came to dealing with church offenses and difficult situations. She also taught me firsthand how God has specially equipped women and how it clearly shows men where our weaknesses or shortcomings are. Things that women seem to do naturally; we somehow struggle with. They seem to easily display empathy, self-control, patience and just loving on others. It was not what I had in mind for my first assignment in ministry, but in God's wisdom it was exactly what I needed at the time. I will forever feel indebted to her for the many lessons she taught me.

My wife and I both served in the children's ministry under her for a few years before things started to change within the church. It is amazing how much time flew by as we grew to really enjoy serving in that capacity despite the initial disappointment I had. Evangelical churches (and particularly this denomination) are well known for staff changes as people move on to new "callings" all the time. It has always seemed that just about the time the church is growing, things appeared ideal, and the excitement level was at a peak; that it was time for God to shake things up in the leadership. I am not so sure that I wholeheartedly buy into that, but that is how it always seems to go. It is always disappointing and sad for the congregation, yet it also is conveyed in a manner that makes it look like a great opportunity for the leaders to take on a bigger assignment or a bigger church. Change can be difficult anyway, but you learn to cope with it better as a leader because you know it is inevitable in ministry. Sometimes it is a brutal process and other times it is a smooth or natural transition. We stayed for quite a while after this transition but eventually it would be time for us to move on as well.

One of the associate pastors at our church took a position in the state of Washington near Olympia as the senior pastor. Shortly thereafter he invited us to come join the staff and serve with him as an associate pastor. In the beginning it would not be a full-time position as far as pay went, but the expectation was for it to grow into full-time ministry and support. In other words, it would begin as part time pay with full time duties. The overwhelming perspective was for me to understand that it was "a position" regardless of the financial aspects! Accepting this position would require a dramatic change in our lives. One that called for us to leave everything we had known and built in our lives up to this time. My wife would have to leave her full-time work position that she had known for over 20 years. I would have to leave my work as well, which was the highest paying position I had up to that point. And, we would have to sell our house and move over 1500 miles away from home with no family or friends nearby.

Most people thought we were "nuts." The irony that we would be going back to the very area that we had to leave a little more than a decade ago because of being broke and deflated only added to everyone's skepticism. Did they not think we were puzzled or questioning God's sense of irony? I can tell you that we wrestled with it more than they did. We had finally reached a place where we had great jobs, a nice home and what seemed like a normal life. I can see why many people would question why someone would give all that up to journey into the unknown. It was no doubt one of the boldest leaps of faith we have ever taken in ministry. It was scary and exciting at the same time. But things were strangely if not miraculously falling into place that helped to convince us that God was indeed calling us to go and step out in faith.

Unexpectedly, I suddenly had an opportunity to transfer my work positions from Omaha to a manufacturing plant up in Olympia. I would have a good paying job waiting for me if we decided to move, so any financial concerns were miraculously being resolved. So, we decided to fly up to the State of Washington to visit the church. Initially, we felt like we were warmly welcomed, and that God surely was behind this move. We viewed, or should I say revisited the surrounding areas because we were already familiar with a lot of the nearby cities like Tacoma and Seattle since I was stationed near there while I was in the military. My wife had been with me for the last year of my enlistment, so she was also somewhat familiar with the area.

Amazingly, we were introduced to a couple that was in real estate and they somehow found us a beautiful newly built home to lease just 2 miles away from the church if we decided to move. That was a key element because homes in that area were extremely expensive and we certainly could not afford to buy one in that area. Yet, we still would have to sell our current home and that is almost always an anxious event. So, we put up our house for sale and it sold in less than a day for more than we were asking. Every hurdle, challenge and concern were being easily if not instantly resolved. It clearly looked like God was in each step by clearing and confirming the way for us. Even some of the skeptics within our family and circle of friends were amazed. They had to concede that perhaps we were indeed "called" to move. So, we packed everything up in a U-Haul and set out to start our life in ministry.

Although I would be an associate pastor overseeing special ministries, outreach, and teaching; the senior pastor had primarily taken me on due to my abilities and track record in evangelism. Evangelism was a core mission for the denomination they belonged to (the same one as our previous church), yet they were in dire needs of some evangelistic experience and mentoring to lead them. Many people in the congregation embraced the concept of evangelizing or sharing the gospel with the lost, but had somehow developed the idea over the years that the lost were supposed to come to you. They rarely did anything outside of the church to attract or invite visitors other than perhaps those they worked with or knew closely. They may not have realized it but that typically ends up creating a congregation of only those who are like you instead of a more diverse church population. And, eventually you seem to have less and less opportunities or people to invite.

The church was like so many other churches in the United States that identify as evangelical but limit themselves to reaching primarily within the church far more than they reach out. Unfortunately, some Christians seem to think that if you just construct a church building, schedule service, and maybe do a little advertising that somehow the lost miraculously just walk through your doors looking for Jesus and an altar call. That is a rarity if not totally unrealistic for it happening that way and especially in American culture which has been turning away from church attendance for decades. So, we knew that we would have a tough task on our hands to try and create a shift in the mindset and behaviors of this church.

Aside from the tall task of trying to shift the overall mindset towards evangelism there would be numerous other challenges. Our time in ministry at this church and in this geographical area certainly was going to be huge learning experience for us. We encountered things that you just did not face or were not used to seeing in the Midwest. This area was the origin of the "grunge" movement in the late 1980's with bands like Nirvana (Kurt Cobain) and Pearl Jam. We were coming there right around the height of its popularity. Beyond the distorted or murky guitar play was a penchant for lyrics heavily laden with angst or anguish. This catered to a drug culture that leaned toward the heavy or darker sides and even established its own clothing trends.

The entire geographical area was also a home for numerous "religions" or cults like Eckankar, Jehovah Witnesses, Scientology and Neo Paganism. Not to mention those that were even more deeply involved with the occult and witchcraft that we would run into. We found ourselves up against actual demonic possession... and not just oppression. This was stuff you maybe heard about back in the Midwest occasionally, yet never encountered face to face all that much. Eye popping stuff... but invaluable experience if you want to really see what God means in the Bible about evil forces and the spiritual realm. It is real and quite frankly even a bit intimidating to minister in those situations. And that was just what was happening outside the church.

We would discover that in many ways, the inside of the church was almost as difficult to manage or minister to as the outside was.

We quickly learned that we had joined on to a church that was going through a leadership change and was struggling internally with strife and controlling board members. The church was even grappling with the idea as to whether they would consider continuing as the Pentecostal denomination they started as or perhaps change to non-denominational. Some board members were determined to hold the church hostage and thoughts of a church split or dissolution were considerably possible. The level and frequency of disagreement made it a huge challenge to conduct weekly services let alone think about moving forward or implementing change. Sometimes, we wondered why God had brought us over 1500 miles just to experience this or what we had maybe gotten ourselves into. Our senior pastor friend was tremendously supportive, and he did a masterful job of trying to handle these issues; however, we had never been exposed to such spiritual chaos, visible divisiveness and even lack of respect within a church. It was mind blowing and seemed almost overwhelming at times.

Adding to the pressure was the unforeseen discovery that our presence was not really welcomed with the open arms that we thought it was when we had first visited. We took over special ministries and outreach activities and started implementing some new strategies and programs. We began a life controlling series using Neil Anderson's *Victory over the Darkness* material to offer a resource for those dealing with or coming out of life controlling situations (e.g. drug or alcohol abuse, smoking, relationships, etc.). God knows there were plenty of them both inside and outside the church. We held weekly meetings, and to our delight we were actually experiencing some good success with participation numbers and positive outcomes. Unfortunately, many of the church leaders and prominent members looked down upon this population of people and oftentimes dismissed any progress that was being made. The people that were in our groups were disdained, looked down on and oftentimes their issues were publicly discussed or gossiped about.

In addition to special ministry programs, we started a weekly outreach program to inner city Olympia. The downtown area housed most of the homeless, the downtrodden, addicts and other individuals that we liked to call EGR cases (extra grace required) or unlovely folks. We used to label them as "unlovely" because that is how they appear to people in the church that maybe turn their noses up around them or act "snooty" around them. Please resist the temptation to be offended by those terms or act as if those attitudes do not exist in the church because they certainly do. I am just being blatantly honest and transparent with you. Although, we recognized it as a "religious" spirit; we did not openly or freely address it like we would today if we encountered it in our own church. The potential for church offenses in this atmosphere is pretty much guaranteed, but we had so many issues to deal with that we could only address it when things really blew up and demanded attention.

We started ministering in the heart of the city where there were very few resources available and very few churches reaching out to these people. We did not have a building when we first began so we would just reach out to folks right there on the street. At first it was just me and my family as we tried to recruit or persuade people from the church to go with us, but that was an extremely slow process in getting folks excited about reaching out to others. Some were afraid to get out of their comfort zone; some were just afraid of who we were reaching out to and many others unfortunately looked down upon them and saw it as just enabling or encouraging their lifestyle. Ultimately, more and more people joined us though and we were ecstatic about that.

Although the entire church was not necessarily behind us or willing to volunteer; things were indeed changing as a few hearts were changing for the lost and those in need. Some of our volunteers turned out to be tremendous servants with huge hearts and committed to serving regularly. Pretty soon we were able to rotate crews and had some trustworthy folks to stand in for us, so we did not have to be down there every week. A couple of them grew so much and immersed themselves into this ministry that they eventually took over operations years later when we left the church.

At the beginning of the street ministry we initially would offer them something to eat on Sunday mornings, provide some articles of clothing and necessities and just talk with them. We built relationships with a lot of them and as word got out the crowd kept getting bigger and bigger. Amazingly, God provided a space for us indoors free of charge through someone that liked what we were doing even without us asking or searching for one. That was good because it rains like 90% of the time in that area and the crowd was getting bigger and harder to manage. It had grown to the point that we could actually start organizing things a bit and add on to what we were offering or doing.

So, early Sunday mornings, we started offering them something hot to drink or eat, provide even more articles of clothing including warm and dry outerwear as well as an even bigger variety of personal necessities and hygiene products. They now had a place to sit where we could talk with them and we were now able to conduct a small service for those wanting to stay. And then... we would invite them to church. Not many of them wanted to take us up on that which is typical for this type of crowd, but occasionally we would have someone that wanted to come to church. In the world of evangelism this would normally be considered an exciting development and people would praise God for it. Unfortunately, we did not anticipate that bringing them to church would actually create a new problem in the church instead.

You would think that in most instances that bringing someone to church and particularly someone needing Jesus in their life would be a welcomed event, right? However, once we started outreaching and bringing the homeless or needy to church it instigated an almost immediate opposition by church leaders and prominent members that included some of the board members. They may have thought that masking their opposition as concerns for the general congregation's safety or well-being was virtuous but quite frankly their actions were undeniably and noticeably rooted in religion or religious practices. They clearly were guilty of showing favoritism or partiality towards the well-off while openly displaying their disgust for the needy which should not be.[10] It is okay to voice concern for the "safety" of the congregation when it is appropriate, but many people in the church use that as justification for hiding the fear or disdain that they have for an unchurched or unclean population.

We need to be aware of our uncomfortable emotions or fears and rise above them because God "has not given us a spirit of fear." What makes it extremely uncomfortable and inexplicable in the

Christian realm is when people in the church purposely move away from or visibly avoid those invited needy folks during a service. And, even worse than that is the easily heard whispers or gossip that follow a service. No wonder some folks have no desire to ever step foot in a church building again. When the top issue of discussion for the week is not about how great the service was, what the message was about, or what God is doing in your life; and instead is the discomfort of what "kind" of people showed up...then it is evidence of a damaging and dangerous spirit of religion in your midst. The church offenses are likely racking up in numbers even though many do not see it happening at the time.

Although the general atmosphere seemed to be changing a little at a time and there was an increasing acceptance (albeit small acceptance) of the needy people that God was bringing into the church; there was still a noticeable opposition in the congregation to it. I have always been amazed at how the church seemingly knows the words to "Just as I am" or "Come as you are" that have been sung in many Billy Graham Crusades, yet struggles to embrace or apply that concept when it comes time to dealing with it face to face. It is frustrating and troubling for an evangelist like myself. On the other hand, it was extremely gratifying to see some in the church respond in a positive way and illustrate that some spiritual growth was taking place within the church. Even if it was slow or relegated to a few isolated incidences. We knew that we had to try and focus on the positive changes and ignore the peripheral comments and opposition so as to avoid letting the religious outcry win the battle.

That was difficult to do when nearly every step you took was questioned or under attack from someone. And that typically meant one of the prominent leaders or board members. It was exasperating at times because you felt as if you could seemingly never do anything right in their eyes. You could try to approach the conflicts with a humble spirit and even offer unmerited apologies or undeserved respect after being criticized or treated poorly but it did little to appease them or their self-righteous demeanor. Several of them indisputably chose authority and power over any humility or servitude while being a leader. They were in a position of power and somehow felt that everyone needed to be repeatedly reminded of that. It really was shocking to us at the time. But we were somewhat new to the role as a pastoral staff member, so we tried to ignore as much of it as possible and just press on.

The special ministry and outreach ministries that we oversaw were not the only areas that would come under attack. I also taught classes on Sunday mornings before the main service. The senior pastor had wanted us to teach a class to offer more than one option to the congregation. They apparently had an appetite for Sunday School classes with good attendance, but he forewarned me that some of the motives were not entirely pure and that some of them tended to come to Sunday School merely to debate or show off their religious prowess. Oftentimes the class would be right after we had already gone downtown to outreach to the homeless, so I vigorously spent the weekend trying to be well-prepared in advance of the class. We began the class by continuing with their recent series or walk through the Bible. It was a series to examine various books of the Bible one at a time so there was no set timeline or agenda per se. This seemed doable or harmless to me because I felt that I knew the Bible decently enough and was one who not only was in the Word daily, but I had studied it profusely for many years so that I could be a better evangelist and apologist. And, I naively thought that it would be pretty difficult for them to dispute what the Word of God says anyway. However, I would find out just how much I had underestimated what all I was getting into.

I did not realize that I would end up having a couple of board members sitting in on my classes who obviously were there for the sole purpose of critiquing and challenging me. It was very clear in a short amount of time that they were not there for the betterment of the class or to add value to the discussion. Simply and honestly, they were really there just to cause trouble. I can still remember them sitting cross armed in the back of the class eagerly awaiting the start of the class and anticipating a potential debate on scriptural interpretation. Even if they were forced to agree about a certain passage or biblical principle because it was indisputable in the Word; they would still feel compelled to upstage you or publicly affirm that you were correct or got it right this time. Their approach was not like sincere and humble elders that could graciously impart some wisdom or illumination; but rather to belittle you, poke holes in your teachings and offer some liberal or Pacific Northwest interpretation of the scriptures.

One board member would even bring a copy of the *apocrypha* and want to debate scriptural inference as it related or compared to this set of writings. For those of you who don't know what that is, it is a collection of writings or books outside the Old and New Testaments of the Bible that some "religions" try to give equal weight and significance to. Some religions include them as a supplement to their Old Testament books but they are not considered canonical or sufficient for meeting the qualifications of scripture. Although the books or letters are claimed to be by godly men, they were recognized as not being anything above any other human writings or in other words not inspired by God and thus have been largely regarded as non-canonical. Some religions or denominations do find value in including parts or all of them in with their Bibles but that's nothing profound when you consider that many books that are not related to religion or Christianity in the least still have some human value.

After the senior pastor addressed it with the board member, he no longer brought it, but he still showed up in class every week to quote from it and debate its equality or relevancy to the Bible. It was a weekly test indeed and an opportunity for me to grow in patience, humility, diplomacy, tact, and self-confidence. As I look back, I think that I was able to handle that test quite well from an outwardly appearance most of the time. But inwardly it was not a pleasant experience. I have taught now for well over 30 years and I enjoy and love teaching in a variety of venues or contexts. I have looked forward to teaching assignments with excitement and anticipation, but I cannot say that I was looking forward to this class in this particular instance. Sometimes, I actually dreaded Sunday mornings and would have preferred to just go do outreach with the homeless. But I endured it and tried to focus on helping others in the class amidst all the rhetoric, spin on scripture and unnecessary sidebars.

The funny thing about it is that those classes were actually a "piece of cake" compared to some of the board meetings I had to attend. Those were nearly always filled with some large dispute and they seemed like an anticipated opportunity for some members to challenge the new senior pastor regardless of whether the grievance was relevant or not. Some meetings included animated outbursts, obvious attempts to intimidate or even threaten the pastoral staff and even instances that you could arguably call "blackmail" by threatening to disclose information publicly to the congregation if they did not get their way. I had never seen anything like it in my life. Let alone in the church.

I was amazed that the senior pastor did such a good job with self-control and handling some of the behaviors. I am sure that I could not have displayed the same cool manner as the senior leader and would have probably resigned long before him. Or, I quite possibly would have been relieved from my duties for wanting to shake some sense into them. My fear of not being able to sufficiently control my tongue or behavior caused me to just remain silent most of the time except for those times where I felt that I had to speak out. Those few times that I felt compelled to exhort them to consider Christian character and maintain some level of decency were met with predictable scorn and despising responses. At times it felt like my dream of ministry was suddenly turning into a nightmare. I often wondered, "what had I done and what predicament had I put my family in?" I did not realize at the time, but I was accruing an inventory of church offenses that would ultimately surface and clearly show the damage from them when combined with other offenses years later.

Nonetheless, despite the contention and constant opposition we tried to carry on and obediently persevere in hope of eventual change to the church atmosphere. Although, the tension and strife within the church was noticeably evident, it was not enough to surpass or cancel all the good that God was doing. The special ministries, outreach, and daily opportunities to evangelize were all flourishing. So much was happening outside of the church that we were sure it would ultimately have to have a positive impact on the inside of the church. Although I did wonder that if it were not for the constant opposition from church leaders how much more things could or would have grown in the church.

In our last year of ministering in that church the senior pastor felt that it was finally time to introduce them to home fellowship groups. They had been highly successful back in Omaha, but success is always somewhat dependent on having good leaders. It took us quite a while to get to a place where we thought we had discipled and developed enough strong leaders before considering the start of them. When we reached that point, we prepared to launch several groups. As one might of thought in a church environment like this you can expect that many of the groups would cling to their close relationships and we would have some challenges with cliques and exclusive groups. Be that as it may, that still happens even in good church environments, so it is not something unique to that church or area. As a leader you just need to be aware of it in advance and work on ultimately growing those groups out. The groups were successful in many ways and it seemed like we might have actually been on the precipice of some badly needed spiritual growth in the areas of community, honoring one another and growing a healthy body of believers.

Our home group was growing the fastest out of all of them which was an exciting event, but anyone associated with home groups knows that you don't want them growing too fast before you have developed some potential leaders and can confidently split up a group. Part of our fast growth was attributed to the fact that we had many of the people with evangelistic hearts, so folks were always inviting someone. Our group also included some of the homeless and needy families from the outreach ministry. It was growing so fast that we soon had to stop holding the group in our home and move to one of our members' homes that was much larger and could handle a bigger crowd. We also soon discovered that we were starting to get some nomadic attendees. Those leaving other groups to come join ours. That can quickly become a problem and create tension or friction amongst groups, so we discussed as a staff that on occasion we would need to kindly decline the switch between groups and encourage or steer them in a different direction.

Another problem we discovered is how everyone wanted to send us some of their un-discipled or harder cases to work with. Some felt ill-equipped to handle them and yet others plainly did not want them in their groups. Reaching out to the lost and those needing extraordinary care was apparently still too much for some of them to take on just yet. Although, some of those instances included board members who should have been spiritually mature enough to handle them but likely just did not want the burden of having them in their group. We realized that we still had a problem with some folks in the church that had difficulty in accepting others as they were and not wanting to put in the effort to disciple them or care for them.

Basically, those groups and leaders wanted "the fish cleaned" before bringing them into their groups. If you are not familiar with the concept of "uncleaned fish", it is a common term or phrase in ministry that refers to someone who made a commitment to Christ, but is not discipled or has overcome some of their worldly issues just yet. It is an elaboration of metaphor when Jesus said he would make the disciples "fishers of men."

Some of those groups and leaders wanted to send us all their uncleaned fish as they preferred to have groups that already had mature or discipled believers. They thought our group was better equipped to handle them and that it must have been God's design to create the groups that way. Of course, we would take them in, but this did not help the church body to get out of their comfort zones or learn to minister to all groups of people. This seemed like a mountainous if not impossible task to get them to change the way that they viewed the unchurched. Trying to constantly overcome the religious attitude in the church was wearing us out over time. And the church offenses initiated by the "religious" leaders only continued to mount. Not just the ones against us but against other vulnerable people in the body as well.

After two years of battling with all the issues in this church and being so far away from home; it started to weigh heavily on my wife and family. Probably me as well. Although, the Bible tells us that God will not force you to be tempted or endure "more than you can bear"; we oftentimes wonder if He is paying close attention while we suffer and seemingly reach our limit. We were so far away from any family members that we had not seen most of them for years now. Our lease on the home was ending and we started to pray and consider whether we were supposed to stay or return home. We still had ongoing opposition or resistance in the church that was led by many of the board members and although some things got better over time; that conflict was still noticeable and influential on the rest of the body. Essentially, anything outside of their own ideology could expect to be challenged or quashed. And, now all of a sudden, a new element or issue arose where the church was encountering even more difficult times. The church secretary was suddenly caught having an affair and she was married to one of the board members, so you can imagine the amount of new controversy within the church. In the end we felt that with all the circumstances involved, we had done all that we were called to do and that it was time to return home to Nebraska.

Though our first full-time ministry position was perhaps the most challenging experience we had with the church up to this point and might even sound disastrous to you; it provided experiences that have proven to be invaluable and contributed greatly to our accumulation of wisdom and discernment over the years. It was a great training ground that simply cannot be duplicated or experienced in other parts of the United States. The experiences contributed greatly towards a tremendously greater understanding of spiritual warfare and the forces of evil. It took a toll on us no doubt, but it also blessed us with some of the best evangelistic training, experiences, and opportunities that we ever encountered in our years of ministry.

We had opportunities to work directly with great men in ministry like Neal Anderson and Luis Palau. We were used to help lead thousands to Jesus Christ during our time up there. We had unprecedented favor in reaching the homeless and pioneering some of the first street ministry activity to take place in Olympia, Washington. We were blessed to serve alongside some great servants who truly had a heart for God and for the lost. We were even more blessed to serve under a great senior pastor who supported us and was a great mentor. And, we made some great friends in the Lord that still exist today.

Despite all the church offenses (too many to include all of them specifically), trials, tribulations, challenges, and growing pains... we felt that it was worth it in the end to be doing what God had appointed us to do. The only problem (and it would prove to be a big one) was that most of those church wounds would be tucked away deep inside of us only to surface years later and attach themselves to newer offenses. That would unfortunately and unknowingly brew to result in a disastrous and crippling impact on my call to ministry.

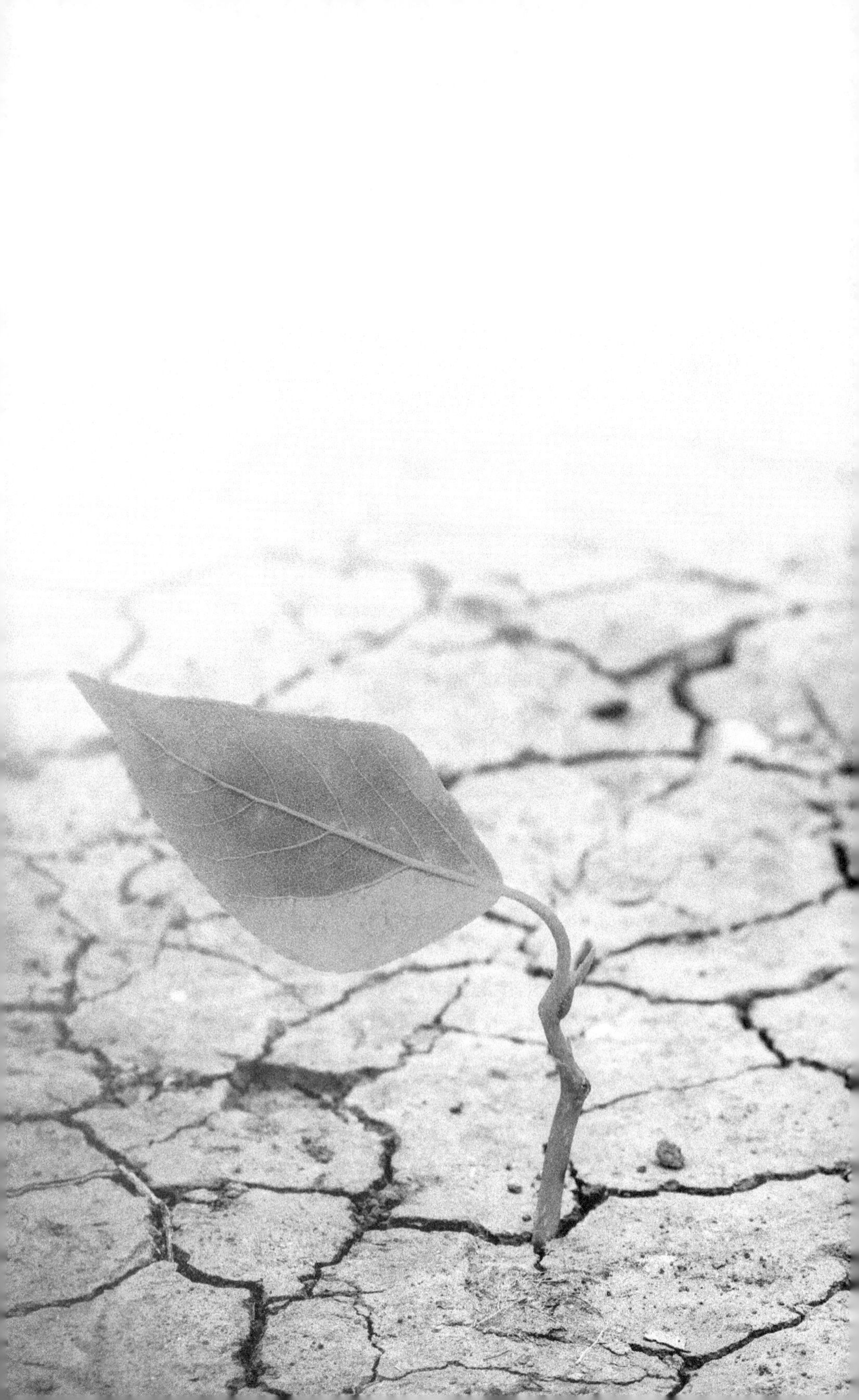

6

WONDER YEARS

"Taking the church to the community but leaving the churchiness at home."

After moving back home to Nebraska we knew that we would need to take some time to pray and try to figure out what God intended for us to do next. And...of course, we knew that we also needed at least a little bit of time to heal. We were a bit naïve about church wounds back when we first started in ministry, so as I have looked back over the years I know that we did not take enough time nor give the attention to those wounds which needed to be reconciled and mended. In some ways, I disregarded some of the experiences and laughed them off as if they really did not have a serious impact or cause any real damage. Little did I know then just how much damage had actually been done.

I wish that I were a bit more savvy, experienced, and prepared to deal with that spiritual realm back then, as I could have possibly eliminated or at least minimized the impact that those offenses ultimately had on me and my family. I was too flippant about counting it as mere bizarre church behaviors by the leaders rather than realizing how those wounds could be deceivingly hidden.

They stayed secluded in my spirit until the enemy would chose an opportune time to bring them back up, causing things to boil over in the future. Sadly, I believe that many young ministers naively treat offenses with the same nonchalant attitude as I did and end up casually chalking it up to just the typical perils of ministry. Unfortunately, they will likely have to endure a period in their life and ministry where some level of damaging consequence comes to light.

As we were healing and praying for direction; we needed to also figure out where we would attend church in the interim. It was not as if we had not prayed and discussed God's plan prior to leaving the church in Washington state, but we did not have clear direction before leaving. To those who have sometimes felt the same way sometimes, you can be assured that others wrestle with trying to get clear cut directions. I will tell you that it does not always just simply fall into place. You may have to go with what you do know, like we did. We did not have all the answers, but we knew that it was time for us to leave. So, we went back to what we had called our home church prior to leaving for ministry. We weren't sure if this is where we needed to be in interim, but it seemed like a natural assumption or the right thing to do since they were an integral part of launching us into full-time ministry. We thought it would be a safe place for us until we felt like we were concretely and clearly hearing from God.

We went to visit the church and attend their services on the first Sunday after our return. Obviously, we were overjoyed to see a lot of old friends. People we had served with and the church environment that we had grown to love and appreciate for so many years. We had heard that they were going through another leadership change, but we had been a part of so many of those that it really seemed of no consequence to us at the time.

Some churches keep the same leadership at the top for years if not decades, however the denomination we were a part of was somewhat notorious for changes. Leaders continuously felt called to new ministries or new churches. A large part of this was because they planted so many new churches that the dynamics of church growth and new church plants seemed to inherently call for changes. A denomination that aggressively plants new churches can expect rapid and perpetual changes in each church as their needs quickly grow. This church had just changed leadership a few years ago when we had left to go minister up in Washington but certainly it was not entirely out of the ordinary.

Changes in church leadership invites a variety of responses. Sometimes, the change can seem so natural and expected that the transition and acceptance by the congregation are almost seamless and uneventful. Other times a change in leadership can cause a wide array of emotions, perspectives, and reactions to surface. There can be a noticeable divisiveness and display of animosity between populations in the church that see the change differently. Oftentimes this is evidenced by their strong opinions and visible opposition to some elements of the change. It is an atmosphere that is ripe for producing church offenses and wounds. It can be anything but a smooth transition and sometimes even include disastrous events. Unfortunately, the latter scenario is what was taking place at our church that we returned to.

We were not aware of the disposition or the temperature of the church environment ahead of time, so we really had no idea of any ongoing tension or struggles. Evidently, there were some in the church who were still tremendously hurt merely because of the change in leadership. That is not all that uncommon as people become closely attached and comfortable with their pastors. But feeling hurt can invite a lot of emotions and undesirable reactions. Because of the unexpected transition, those that were hurting felt strongly about moving slowly through the process rather than evaluating or considering new candidates right away. The church apparently had already interviewed and invited several candidates in the past few weeks. Those that were still hurting from the announced change were in favor of slowing things down and perhaps tabling the voting of any new candidates for a while. However, another part of the church felt they had already achieved due process and felt that within the group of potential candidates there was somebody that was indeed called to take over leadership. And... of course, both sides felt they were the ones hearing from God. We had no idea that there had already been some friction and mounting tension within the past few weeks during the candidate process. Nor that this service was targeted to try and answer many of the concerns that both sides held. We were in for a bit of a surprise.

Service started normally and that meant kicking things off with some lively praise and worship. Everything would have seemed normal to most folks visiting, but I could tell and feel that something was not right. A strange heaviness or spiritual barrier in the sanctuary. I don't profess to have all or even most of the spiritual gifts that the Bible lists, but I can tell you that I have always been able to walk into a place and recognize when there is an overwhelming or special presence of the Holy Spirit. This might sound strange to some of you, but I can "smell" when it is so intense and special. Interesting and strange perhaps but smell is one of our senses God gave us and the Bible actually talks about the "fragrance" of the Lord.

My instincts would be proven accurate in a very short time. During worship, someone began to publicly speak in tongues. If you are unfamiliar with this you should understand that the manifestation of publicly speaking in tongues doesn't happen every week in a Pentecostal church, but it can and does happen frequently. Or, at least it used to. My wife and I were both extremely familiar with it in the church. Like many others, we have spoken in tongues in our personal lives since being "Baptized in the Holy Spirit" but publicly speaking out loud in church is a different spiritual phenomenon. It is one of the gifts mentioned in the Bible and coincides with someone else having the ability or gift to interpret the tongues. It is always supposed to be for the purpose of "edifying" or building up the church. Even corrections by God are still given within His entire character that includes love, grace, and mercy. Unless of course, they are a direct confrontation between Him and evil or wickedness.

So, just because someone spoke out in tongues there was nothing that seemed out of the ordinary, yet other than I still did not have a sense of the overwhelming and confirming presence of the Holy Spirit. And I have pretty much "always" known ahead of time when someone was going to most likely speak out whenever I first walk into a sanctuary. At least for the last twenty years or so anyway. I do not propose to entirely understand why I have this adeptness and I am quite sure that I am not alone in this strange ability; it is just something that God has given me over the years. I do not always have an interpretation, but I seemingly do know when and if it is going to happen. I have reckoned that it is most likely some gift of discernment for me (and surely others) to be able to validate and be certain of the origin of the Word.

After this person spoke in tongues, someone began to interpret. It was still in line with how it normally happens; however, in this instance it was almost immediately noticeable that the interpretation was not an edifying or encouraging word. It was a chastisement and admonishment of some singled-out population of people within the church. Its tone and harsh condemnation were a noticeably and overly authoritative rebuke of some distinct individuals in the church. They were also clearly on the verge of calling out specific people publicly or making them easily identifiable. I had rarely run into an abuse of public tongues up to this point and never to this degree of animosity.

Although, some people may be quick to point out that the Bible does give a few examples of God admonishing His people as an attempt to defend the possibility of a rebuke or condemnation through tongues; it must be noted that those examples are indeed rare occurrences and they were generally directed at God's people as a whole. They were not for the purpose of shaming, condemning, and isolating someone individually or just a few people within the population. The few examples provided in the Bible are primarily in the Old Testament well before the evolution of the church and the gifts of the Holy Spirit. Any admonishments or rebukes given were typically by a well-recognized prophet or special person in the Bible. Thus, God's clear trust of only a few individuals and the absence of a clear-cut emphasis in the New Testament should serve as an extreme caution to all of us. At the very least in regard to giving an admonishing Word in public. It is an extraordinarily sensitive, if not delicate area that can cause a lot of damage. Especially when it is so blatantly derogatory towards just a small population that merely disagrees with a non-doctrinal issue. Someone supporting an interpretation or message that is outside of God's character has an impossible challenge in trying to theologically prove its validation or authenticity.

Even for me and my wife it was a shocking and almost a time-stopping moment. Just about the time you think you have seen everything in ministry; some new example or experience pops up and catches you by surprise. To some or even many, this incident would have seemed bizarre. And, especially to any new visitors. As you might imagine, this initiated some immediate responses and a flurry of activity as the leaders of the church tried to regain some control over the service and shut down the vocal responses and subsequent rebukes. The interim pastor (an older, wiser gentleman and a great friend of ours) had to step in and not only gain control, but try to provide some explanations as to what had just happened. They ultimately were able to continue the service and even have some discussion about the candidate process, but a lot of damage had been done and who knew how irreparable some of it was. It was definitely not the same church that we had left years ago, yet it was a clear illustration of how no church is immune from being vulnerable to the pitfalls of a dependence upon religious spirit and human intellect rather than truly trusting and submitting to God. Regardless of their reputation or past works.

It is almost needless to say that we determined that it was not part of God's plan for us to return to our home church at that particular time. Not because we were afraid of the situation or had some offense ourselves due to what happened. Certainly, we had just come out of much more difficult if not bizarre circumstances that exceeded the discomfort of just one out-of-order service. But we were needing to seek God's plan for ourselves regarding ministry and we needed an environment where we could place our attention solely on seeking that. We loved that church and would have loved nothing better than to remain and maybe even help people going through the difficult time, but we knew God wanted us to maintain our focus on the future and specifically what plans He had for us. It is a good thing that we had initially only set our hearts on just visiting so as not to be disappointed. We were sad for them, but not hurt or severely tainted in our thoughts. It was just unfortunate. So, we prayed and discussed potential options for the immediate future.

One of the benefits or assets in associating with a larger evangelical denomination is that there are plenty of local churches. For the most part you are generally spared from the concerns and questions surrounding their doctrine or what the church believes in. Thus, we were fortunate in avoiding the agonizing process of "looking for a church" that so many people regrettably must go through. We decided to attend one of the sister churches in the area that we were at least somewhat familiar with. They were on the other side of town but because of the closeness of the denomination and affiliated local churches, we had worshipped together with them at times and collaborated on many city-wide events. They were a large church about the same size as our home church and had been established in the community for many years. We knew many of the leaders and the worship style, so we pretty much knew what to expect when we walked through the doors. What we did know, is that we were able to immediately confirm that this was where we needed to be and where God wanted us for now. That was a huge weight off our spirits and one we did not expect to happen so quickly.

This church was not difficult to get connected to and our past relationships with the staff allowed us to start serving right away. We did not join the staff; however, we did become leaders almost immediately. Despite being an established church, a big church always still has needs and areas they need people to serve in. And, because we knew several key leaders our reputation and credibility helped provide the necessary trust for taking over an area of ministry. We were introduced to the youth pastor who also served as pastor over the areas of outreach and evangelism. He was a fast paced energetic and passionate guy who had more stamina than you can imagine. People who know me and know the level of passion that I have had for evangelism would be amazed and much more impressed with his level of energy and passion. I have never met anyone else like him. He was totally serious and committed about truly seeing his "entire" city come to know Jesus. He was raring to go but he had not found someone yet that he could trust to take over the areas of evangelism and outreach that would perhaps lighten his load a bit and help him to focus primarily on the youth. The timing and circumstances were perfect for allowing us to take on this role.

Thus, under his leadership and direction we became the leaders over the evangelism and outreach ministries. We were not only a good fit for this leadership position, but it was the perfect fit for us as well. We received such great support and encouragement and we were allowed to seek a vision for continued expansion of the activities and opportunities. He had already done a tremendous amount of work in establishing some key relationships outside of the church that enabled access to potential witnessing venues like jails, prisons, and youth detention facilities where we would be able to expand the opportunities. Although he was much younger than I; he proved to be a fantastic mentor of sorts.

He graciously poured into me all that he had learned and was always onboard or supportive to take things even further.

We soon found out that he had such a great platform with the senior pastor and elders that practically anything we wanted to do or that was needed for ministry would be easily obtained, along with their backing and financial support. It was an amazing time for us to go from non-stop roadblocks or opposition in our last assignment to having overwhelming support and encouragement. The excitement and backing of the leadership greatly contributed to an overwhelming success of recruiting volunteers and igniting a fire and a passion throughout the larger congregation to reach outside the church walls. We almost never lacked in the number of people wanting to serve or get plugged into evangelism and those ministries. And we needed a lot of volunteers for some of the big events we held.

We took what he had already started and began to build on it. He had gotten some access to the girl's state detention center in Geneva and to the new boy's maximum-security prison in Omaha that allowed for occasional chapel services. We discovered that we were progressively gaining trust and favor with the administrations. So much so, that we could soon expand our opportunities to weekly services and beyond. These evolved from just normal chapel services to include more radical events like outdoor festivals with live bands, games, food, gifts and of course the gospel message. Some of them lasted for hours and were like an all-day carnival atmosphere. That is an amazing opportunity that you may not fully grasp if you are not familiar with how tightly run corrections facilities are. We were even allowed to conduct a special Christmas service for the inmates at the boy's prison and provide Christmas cookies and small gifts for the boys. That was never allowed, yet we miraculously received the necessary support and approval from the warden himself.

The church had some tremendous resources. They had a vibrant young adult internship and discipleship program. They possessed amazing musical, drama, and creative arts skills. We were able to tap into and utilize those resources. The correctional institutions allowed us to take in dynamic worship bands and even some radical, if not cutting-edge musicians or bands that could capture the attention and interest of the young detainees. The interns performed emotional dramas and even entertainment aspects like feats of strength or breaking bricks. The youthfulness of our volunteers or performers could also connect with the young people that were incarcerated in a way that adults simply could not.

All the music and creative presentations we were able to provide were giving us an extraordinary opportunity to share the gospel and lead young girls and boys to the Lord. I cannot tell you how many made a commitment over the years as we never kept track. But it was a lot. And the significance of even one soul would go beyond the importance of any final tally anyway. This really was unprecedented for the corrections in the State of Nebraska to allow some of these things. We could not believe how much leeway and favor we were given. God seemed to open the doors wide for us. As we continued building relationships with the wardens and directors running these places; the potential possibilities continued to increase. Many of those that were incarcerated stayed in contact with us even after their release. These services were obviously significant events in their lives.

This ministry was growing at a rapid pace. So fast that we had to establish a training program for others to get certified access and take responsibility over some of the scheduled visits, so we could give some attention to all the other things that we were implementing. Training people to do jail or prison ministries may have been the most difficult aspect of our ministry. The correctional facilities or prisons are so much different than street witnessing, outreaches to the community or altar calls in the church. The harsh reality is that these people are going to still be behind bars when you pick up and leave after your event or church service. They are left wondering how their life is actually going to change much or possibly get any better while still behind bars. You have some serious psychological hurdles to overcome that truly take the power of God to convince them that He is not only real, but that He wants to be an active part of their life. Most of them carry extraordinary baggage to begin with, and things do not just fall into place or in proper perspective merely because you happen to quote them a few of your memorized scriptures. You have to be a good encourager and an even better evangelist. We had to change the mindset and thinking of our volunteers to understand that the gospel is supposed to be "good news" and they need to be able to share with the inmates that God loves them and still wants an active relationship with them despite whatever it is that they have done or what their consequences are.

Many of the volunteers did not begin with a full understanding of the two most important components involved with jail or prison ministry. The first important aspect is the necessary "commitment" to the ministry. You must be consistent and show up when you say you are going to show up. They have seen a ton of ministries or volunteers come into the prisons and start out with a passion only to fizzle out in a short amount of time. Why on earth would they want to answer another chapel call only to find out that you have abandoned them like so many others? Those that cannot commit to a regularly scheduled obligation and commit to it for a period of time are not ideal candidates for this type of ministry. Sure, nearly everyone moves on in ministry at some point, but this ministry requires more than just an occasional desire to help out every now and then. At least for those who plan on sharing the gospel and are not merely a guest performer or helper for special events.

The other important component is understanding the unique atmosphere you are in when it comes to presenting the gospel. Some volunteers began with an ideology that these inmates needed to grasp the gravity of what they had done and that there are consequences (like prison) for their actions. And they feel it is their job if not their obligation to share those thoughts with the individuals that are incarcerated. The problem is that inmates know consequence better than you could ever explain it to them. Every time that you have finished a service and get ready to leave; they are not going anywhere. And they live in a daily environment that non-believers outside of the prison walls are not confined to. Although God loves a servant's heart and someone who is willing to volunteer; He does not need your help in reminding folks just how bad of a sinner they are. That is the Holy Spirit's job.[4] They will indeed come to grips with the gravity, if not the depravity of their sin as the Holy Spirit convicts them.

Ultimately many of them will open up after a while when they feel comfortable with you or learn to trust you. The methods for sharing the gospel that some new volunteers embraced (like beating them over the head with the Bible) were no doubt a part of their evangelism training somewhere else. Their approach may have even somewhat worked in other environments; but I can tell you that it will not work in jails and prisons. At best, they may just respond or tell you what you want to hear. At worst... you may never see them again or get another opportunity with them.

For some volunteers it was a struggle to understand or embrace the concept of providing the gospel without first incorporating some level of well-intentioned but inappropriate condemnation. Yet, plenty of others understood the difference and excelled at it. Those that struggled still felt they needed to be sure that the person making a commitment was sincere. As if they could really gauge their sincerity. Judging someone's sincerity is not their job anyway. That is up to the Holy Spirit to evaluate. Those types of overzealous volunteers did not realize that they were actually committing church offenses against the inmates. And, I can tell you that they did not serve on our team if they could not overcome those tendencies. You do not have to be in a church to produce or to be inflicted with a church offense. It just becomes a "Church" offense instead with a capital "C", which simply means that it is still the body of Christ or the body of believers that inflict wounds upon others. Being willing and humble enough to serve in this special manner is how you know if you have been called to this specific area of ministry or not.

An important reason for why I am sharing all these details with you about this specific ministry is not because it was challenging for us to operate in this manner, but rather that it was difficult for many people that came to us wanting to volunteer for this ministry. It did not pose any church offense potential against us, but it did occasionally cause offense or hurt feelings for those wanting to volunteer occasionally. And, if they did not abide by our guidelines or expectations, they stood a real good chance of causing a church offense against an inmate.

Some individuals did not like the idea that they were not able to just sign up and get involved with this area of ministry because they "had a heart for it." Others did not agree about specific approaches to presenting the gospel in this unique atmosphere and wanted to debate the effectiveness of hammering home a message. And, still others just seemed to have a hard time submitting to any kind of authority. That cannot happen in a jail or prison environment where authority is king. The bottom line is that the offenses some volunteers might have perceived as coming from us or that they may have held against us; were actually steeped in their own religious spirit and the past overly religious practices that they were used to. If you are one reading this book and the circumstances sound familiar to you; perhaps this portion sheds some light on the important aspects of this topic for you. If not, I would encourage you to pray and ask God why it is a point of contention for you.

All this aside, I want to point out that we were tremendously blessed with an abundance of great volunteers that genuinely loved reaching out to the young people behind bars and they loved sharing the gospel. They undoubtedly reaped great rewards in heaven because of their hearts for serving and willingness to step aside and let God be in control of the life changes. The instances of those people who might have taken offense at our approach or disagreed with us in some way were rare and yet we knew it was necessary discernment.

We have always been associated with this area of ministry to various degrees over the years. Even after we left this church for our other church assignments. This specific ministry became very near and dear to our hearts. I have missed it tremendously over the years but understand why God moved us on to other ministries and roles. When we left, God filled the voids that were created with other great servants that were totally capable of shouldering the responsibility. There is no way for us to know the level of impact it will have on the many young girls and boys that were exposed to the gospel because of God's grace, mercy, and miraculous intervention; but I would imagine it will prove to be huge over time. God opened up the doors of opportunity beyond all imagination. Usually, that means the Holy Spirit was orchestrating some tremendous spiritual changes. I have great hope about the seeds that were planted because I know the impact that the gospel message and the work of the Holy Spirit had on my own life. Those spiritual changes stayed with me no matter how far I strayed and helped to bring me back to the church years later.

In addition to the detention, jail, and prison ministries we were simultaneously busy with organizing and coordinating outreach events. These were events targeting various areas of the community. Although they were mostly strategic parts of the city like the housing projects, downtown areas, and homeless shelters, we would also do them for just the local general community. Many of these outreaches involved a radical mindset that considered the cultural influences outside of a church environment. Taking the church to the community but leaving the churchiness at home. Not leaving God at home; just the religiosity and any close-minded attitudes. No, we did not compromise our Christian character and indulge in worldly behaviors. We just reached out to them with a sense of normal human interaction and utilized the resources God had given us.

Most of the outreaches included some combination of bouncy houses, games, prize giveaways, clowns, balloons, face painting and various food or treats. Many of them had live bands and loud music playing throughout. Volunteers that manned booths helped to meet the public's needs through passing out hygiene essentials, health screenings, or bagged food. Some of these were huge operations and even costly to be honest. Others were as simple as taking popsicles or a grill and hotdogs to the housing projects during the summertime just to connect with folks and possibly witness to some. Either way, we always had the full support of the church including finances. They believed so much in investing in the community and evangelism that all they had to do was take an offering and we always had more than what we needed. Even when we included expensive giveaways like bikes, stereos, and gift cards for groceries. Nothing had to come out of the general fund. We were always careful to spend just as much if not more in the poorer neighborhoods as we would spend in more affluent ones. Sometimes we even collaborated with other churches to combine resources and volunteers while simultaneously building strong relationships with them.

You should know that these were not just our great and wonderful ideas. Luis Palau and others had been doing huge outreaches like this or even bigger ones for years and exposed us to the possibilities at one of his crusades up in Olympia, Washington. Our outreaches were never close to the impressive scale that Luis and some others do, but nonetheless they were still very large events and they had not previously been done too much in our hometown area. You should know that it is okay to borrow ideas from others in the Church. You do not have to invent or create everything independently of everyone else. God owns all of the ideas and approaches anyway and the evangelists that I know are always more than happy to share ideas that work.

Outreaches were a tremendous amount of fun and it gave us the opportunity to witness to people in a variety of ways. Much of it was just the opportunity for face to face contact and discussion with those in the community. Sometimes it would lead to a commitment or request for prayer. Oftentimes we would incorporate the testimonies of gang members, drug dealers and abortion survivors between bands or music intervals that also effectively connected with some audiences. All of these interactions were either connected to the gospel themselves or a prelude to preparing for sharing the gospel on a larger scale sometime near the end of the event. Frequently, we were bold enough and fortunate enough to share the gospel right out in the open and in the public areas of the city. We have no idea once again how many people had made commitments because we just were not personally into keeping numbers. However, we were aware that churches do like to know those sorts of things (even ours), so we still tried to provide our best estimates without necessarily using precise tracking. We just know it was a lot of people that we were able to reach out to and a lot of individual souls that personally connected with Jesus!

In addition to the ministry to detention centers, prisons, and the various outreaches; I was afforded the opportunity to teach regular classes on evangelism. This is probably where I first fell in love with teaching. In truth, I love preaching and teaching both. Not everyone can do both, but I found out that God had gifted me to do so, and it has come in handy as I have been able to minister in a variety of settings and contexts. Oftentimes, teaching is necessary where preaching may fall short. Preaching can drive home a message with the help of the Holy Spirit, but some witnessing scenarios, Bible studies or classroom genres require someone to break down scripture or the Gospel message in a manner that is suitable or understandable for those being discipled. Preaching can also fire folks up, but it is typically more rhetorical or presented as a one-way delivery with little to no interaction other than the occasional "Amen" or "Praise the "Lord." I love the interactive component with the audience that teaching offers.

Teaching affords the opportunity to break things down practically for people and encourages the audience to critically think about topics like evangelism, apologetics, and the Bible. In the religious genre, teaching is utilized to dissect information and search deeper into a topic. Teaching evangelism classes allowed me to introduce the participants to a wide array of personalities of both older and contemporary evangelists. And, it offered the opportunity to explore their methods or perspectives on evangelism. Historic pastors and evangelists like Spurgeon, Billy Sunday, Smith Wigglesworth, Luther, Wesley, Calvin, Whitfield, Torrey, Dwight Moody and of course the apostle Paul. Contemporary ones like Ravi Zacharia, Billy Graham, Louis Palau, Ray Comfort and many more. People that find themselves stuck on just "one way" to preach the gospel would undoubtedly be enlightened by studying some of these great men of God and discovering their different personalities, methods, and approaches. Even more importantly, is the chance that you would be able to discover how God has miraculously used each one of them!

This class environment was nothing like what we had experienced in Washington as people were excited and more eager to learn or discuss topics than debate or show off their level of knowledge. Instead of learning or ascribing to just one way of presenting the gospel we explored all the many ways to share it in a variety of scenarios with an emphasis of leaning on the Holy Spirit rather than ones' own expertise. Yes, we covered traditional and important approaches like using the Bible for Roman's Road or the Book of John, the bridge, the use of tracts or story evangelism. We also covered other important aspects that the participants needed to consider like lifestyle evangelism, avoiding the temptation to argue or prove God's existence, being overzealous or pushy, and method versus message. It may very well have been my biggest accomplishment because it helped to develop a number of potential evangelists and equipped a lot of church members that have since taken the gospel to others well-beyond what I was capable of doing on my own.

As this chapter comes to a close, I think you can probably see why I named this chapter the Wonder Years. It was some of our best times in ministry and especially for such a long stretch of success and blessing. I am sure that the church was not completely devoid of any really damaging offenses that went beyond some getting their feelings hurt; but there could not have been very many during that time frame and they certainly were not happening around us. It was a welcome reprieve from the controlling, oppositional and antagonistic environment we had come from. We did not realize it at the time but it was also an essential time of spiritual rest that effectively energized us in preparation for the land mines and hornet's nest that we were about to unknowingly face.

7

THE GOOD, THE BAD AND THE UGLY

After several years of overseeing and further developing the areas of evangelism, outreaches, and prison/corrections ministries at that church; we were suddenly faced with a difficult decision. I was asked to consider a staff position as an associate pastor at a church where a friend of ours had just became senior pastor at. We had worked with him years ago at our home church when he was the youth and evangelism pastor there. Now, he had just taken over as senior pastor at a church close to home in Iowa and there was a lot of overhaul and restoration to do. He knew our familiarity with difficult situations like the church in Washington and was needing some help with a tough church environment.

It was a difficult decision because we enjoyed what we were doing, and we were experiencing tremendous results as well as infinite support from the church in providing whatever we needed. But we were still just leaders that were volunteers per se, and we knew at some point God would call us again for a deeper role. However, the remembrance of the bad experiences that we went through at the church up in Washington were still in the back of our minds and I wondered if we wanted to go through something like that again, regardless of the spiritual dividends that are to be had when overhauling a church. It was not an easy decision, and even though we took time to pray and consider it, the decision would still be a difficult one in the end no matter the outcome. They were both appealing in their own ways. Despite that things were going great where we were, we knew that just because something is flourishing it is not always part of God's equation when asking you to make a move. As a matter of fact, that seems to be a common time of when He moves you.

So, in the end we felt it was a door opening into a ministry commitment for us again. I know the saying that God can use you wherever you are at and I believe that He can "use all things for the good", even when you make bad decisions or miss His intentions somehow. However, I wanted to try and get it right. Especially considering the events from the last time my wife and I joined a staff. To this day, I still do not know that we did get it right. Little did we know what tough times lay ahead at this church. Did we miss God's voice and should have stayed put? Or, did He intend for us to go through all that we went through at this next church? I am not sure.

We joined the staff at this church as an associate pastor overseeing the youth ministry, evangelism, and outreaches. If you have not noticed; I say "we" a lot despite that it may just be me that was on staff or took a particular position. This is because whenever you are in ministry it will involve both you and your wife. Even those instances where a spouse may take a back seat or not necessarily even want to be involved; they are still impacted, and they become a part of that ministry regardless. In my wife's case she has always been an integral and very important part of everything I have done in ministry. People may have seen her doing out front things like leading worship, praying with someone, ministering to the young girls or just being with me at most events. But most people have no idea how much behind the scenes work she has done in addition to those out-front or visible things. Tasks like organizing an event, ordering supplies, organizing the worship, being a hostess, creating a newsletter, oversight at outreaches, invoicing, emailing and yes plenty of cleaning. And...never once in over thirty years has, she received or requested a paycheck for it! That is what I mean when I say God calls both of you regardless of who has the position or title. Unfortunately, they are also a recipient or partner of any church offense that you have to face.

At the beginning of our time in ministry at this church there was plenty of passion, fire or energy and excitement for both us and the church. This was a church that had gone through several pastors in the past few years and pretty soon it became clearly evident why that was. The church had a very controlling board that liked to keep things the way they were in the past and do things their own way. If your vision was not in line with their ideas on how things should be run or was outside of their personal preferences, then it either was not supported or simply denied. We soon discovered that a root cause of this was attributed to the discovery that primarily everything circulated around the "Christian" school that the church owned. All the board members kids were enrolled in the school and many of the board members and their wives also worked at the school. In some ways that might seem honorable or commendable if you took the perspective that they thought so highly of the school that they all wanted to outwardly support it; but the arrangement posed a huge potential for creating a conflict of interest and was wrongfully impacting board decisions.

Another huge problem in that arrangement was that a significant portion of the finances for the school were tied to the general budget of the church. That meant that some peoples tithes and offerings for the church were supporting the school whether their kids attended or not. In my opinion and most likely beyond just my own; this should not happen. I do not see any biblical precedent for using tithes and offerings to manage a school for kids. Especially, if the entire body is not benefiting from it. And, I was quite sure that most people in the congregation were not privy to this arrangement. I do believe that you could take an offering that affords people and opportunity to give if they want, but I do not feel that you should be doing something like this behind the scenes just because you can. Well, you can only imagine the backlash that I received for voicing opposition to the way things were being run since the board members either had all their kids attending or they were longtime and close friends of the other board members who did not have any kids enrolled.

The senior pastor (the friend who had asked me to come serve with him) was aware of this and agreed with me that things needed to change, but he recognized that it would have to be some incremental process to get back on track because otherwise the school would most likely have to abruptly close. The attendance did not generate enough tuition revenue to sustain its operation all on its own. A couple of the board members voiced that perhaps in their spirit they agreed as well that this was not a proper use of the general fund, but they were still unwilling to fully acknowledge it. They instead supported the justification or logic that the funds were being used as an "investment" in young Christians regardless of whether everyone in the congregation chose to take advantage of the opportunity to enroll their kids in a Christian school or not. They further justified it by contending that anyone could reap the same benefits by simply enrolling their kids and enjoying the same discount on tuition as the board members families had. If they could afford to. The failure in that logic would likely be apparent to most individuals who were not blinded by their own implication or their skewed and biased perceptions.

Because the arrangement with the school and its finances drove so much of the church agenda; the board meetings and subsequent decisions reflected that influence. It was extremely difficult for me to attend board meetings because although I was invited as part of the staff, I did not have a vote and only a limited voice. That would have been just fine with me if some of things going on were not taking place. Some members felt that it might be best if I was not even a part of the board meetings. However, several others were worried about the look of impropriety and speculation coming from the congregation if I was no longer allowed to be a part of the meetings. So, I was allowed to continue attending. They did allow me to speak at times, but only if they deemed it useful and supportive of the school. Whenever I felt the need to question or suggest anything that was contrary to their direction or was considered a threat to the school's influence and use of funds then my views were easily dismissed or ignored altogether.

I could not help but reflect on the controlling board in the church that we left in Washington. As appalling as some of their behaviors were back then; this board made the one up in Washington state look almost not so intolerable. I always knew that the church is full of imperfect people including leaders, but I would have never imagined that some of the behaviors and mentalities I was seeing could exist in church boardrooms. Lest you think that my issue is with church boards in general; I had known many board members and elders in the past. I had always viewed them with tremendous respect and considered them great men and women of God. And, I still do. They were people who relied on godly wisdom and biblical principles in and out of boardrooms. I was just not used to an environment that so blatantly or easily ignored the Word of God and the voice of the Holy Spirit as these two boards did. I was not sure just how bad things could get.

Regardless of whether we made the wrong decision or not, we knew that God either had us there for a reason or He was at least well aware of what we had gotten into. We decided that we should just try to have patience in the changes that needed to be made administratively and financially and try to let God work on them in that area now that it had least been uncovered. We realized that it could not just change overnight as the closing of the school would assuredly impact the church as well. So, we tried to just focus on what we needed to do or were called to do with the youth and outreach. Holding back on my frustrations and tempering my views perhaps would take some of the pressure and tension off from being an outspoken outsider who had already stepped on a lot of toes. It seemed like a wise concession; however, it still would not prevent some of that controlling spirit from later seeping into the areas of ministry that we oversaw as well.

The youth did not have their own place or facilities for conducting youth services, youth events or just hanging out. Up to this point they had just joined the adults in the services during the week and had occasional Bible studies or groups. Not too much directly geared towards the youth. We discovered an old storage area that had accumulated a lot of "stuff" over the years but was not really being used for anything other than a dumping zone. The storage had potential for anyone with a vision. It took a lot to convince the board to authorize the use of the space despite that it was not being used for anything else other than housing a lot of clutter that was just taking up space. We were finally allowed to lay claim to the space for the youth but were authorized with little to nothing in finances to help remodel it because the school was being upgraded and absorbed most of any available funds. Even small cost items like paint or cleaning materials was scrutinized with every purchase. We were resolved in using most of our own money just to avoid the anticipated conflict and questioning about every dollar spent. And, we relied on a lot of our friends from outside of church that we knew to help clean up and decorate the space. That was okay though because we were determined to provide a facility specifically for the youth. Nothing extraordinary; just a space they could call their own. Besides, we had fun doing it and it was enjoyable to see it develop and come to life. It also afforded us an opportunity to build new relationships with many of the youth that volunteered to help out.

When we were finished, we had a big main room to primarily be used as a sanctuary for youth services and a smaller room for classes and just hanging out or playing games. One of our friends was an artist and painted a radical mural on the wall over the stage for us with the new youth group name. The name was an issue itself as the board fought with the idea of allowing us to name the youth group something other than what could be tied to the school's vision statement. It was not surprising as pretty much everything had become contested or resisted up to this point. You might say we were getting used to it or at least able to deflect it better. We knew that it was not just us that they opposed because the church had a long history of resistance and control. It had a well-known negative reputation in the community because many people had attended and left over the years and they had no problem in spreading the word about the church's domineering approach.

So, we finally had a place for the youth, but we were lacking a good or at least a complete worship band. Up to this point we had either worshipped with the adults and then went to the youth facility where I would preach a message, or we made do with a keyboardist that could team with my wife to lead worship. I do not want to knock worship as if it is dependent upon all of today's bells and whistles, but it was not dynamic or what we were used to ourselves. And the keyboardist (bless her heart) was stuck in the hymnal book which just was not going to work for the young people all the time. I had conducted worship myself many times in the prisons when I was left no options, but I was not a very good guitar player and an even worse singer. Consequently, we were a bit shorthanded on adequate let alone talented musicians to help with worship.

The church was non-denominational, but it was regarded as a spirit filled church and at one time it was even said to be Pentecostal. Typically, these churches always seem to have a supply of musicians and worship teams including one for the youth ministries. Unfortunately, that was not the case at this church when we started out. Some say they had run most of them off over the years. The adults had pretty good worship because the senior pastor and his wife were gifted in this area; but all the other musicians were committed to playing with them in the adult services being held on the same evening. And the pastor's wife was not open to sharing anyone of them with us. In hindsight, I should have taken notice of that. So, we tried doing a little brainstorming and we came up with the bright idea of holding youth group on a different night. That would allow us to utilize some of their worship team members since it was an off night, but as you might imagine that idea was shot down immediately. They had never done that in the past, and they did not want the youth service to happen on a different night than when the adults were meeting. I could see part of the logic in that, but I also saw the controlling element at work, and I wondered why it was so hard to compromise or want to help the youth out.

Nonetheless, God is always faithful in providing or finding a way even amid opposition. Bit by bit we were being provided with musicians. Our son had been taking drum lessons for a while and although he was young, he could play. He just needed a worship leader to help develop and lead him. We reached out to a young man whose family had been associated with the church for a long time. He would occasionally come to church with his family, but he had become somewhat of an outcast because of his tattooed appearance and secular past. His family had a long rich history with the church, but religious attitudes in the church over the years helped to squash any hope of him serving in the church. Funny how no one ever thought about bringing him alongside and mentoring or discipling him. He was a great guitar player and ironically had his own band that played both secular and Christian heavy metal. We built a relationship with him and he agreed to come help us with worship. Additionally, a friend of ours that used to help us with our outreaches came to help with worship as he could sing, play guitar and the bass. He was a tattoo artist that had spent time in prison, but had found Jesus years ago. Oftentimes he had given his testimony at our outreaches.

Things were all of a sudden coming together and the team was putting together some awesome worship in our services. We had more tattoos on stage than you might see in some biker bars.

They may have not looked the part; however, they were saved, and man could they rock. You probably would not think much of it today if you saw them on stage, but back then their appearance was shocking to some. Especially, people in this congregation. It was not long before the youth worship services were surpassing the environment in the adult services. The enthusiasm and electricity even rivaled the Sunday morning services as the worship team grew and became more skilled. That was a developing problem as some resentment was evident. But it was something the youth had not been exposed to in a long time and it was effectively starting to light a fire. I probably should have saw it coming as it was not long before the board called a special meeting to discuss what kind of characters that we were exposing their kids to.

It certainly would not be the last "special board meeting" that was called on my behalf, but it was one of the more interesting ones that put religion and religious attitudes on full display. The board did not want us to allow the young man we had recruited from the church to lead worship for the youth. They were concerned about his looks, his past, and the level of his commitment to Christ as well as what kind of negative impact it would have on their kids. They were even concerned about old heavy metal bumper stickers he had on his truck and had not yet removed. I pointed out to them that although he might be out front on the stage that it was actually my wife and I who were in charge of the worship and services and he was merely serving. And, just like anyone else he was being discipled by us despite their perceptions as to whether he was worthy of leading worship or not, let alone just being in our services. That did little to appease them or convince them that we knew what we were doing. It did not look like I would be able to easily overcome the religious and pious attitudes in the meeting as it was a bit contentious and one-sided. So, I offered them a deal. I placed my Bible on the table and challenged them to find just one disciple in the Bible that had it all together when Jesus picked them and if they could then I would take him off the stage. You can argue my method if you like as not being very diplomatic or respectful, but it did effectively put an end to the push to remove him from our worship team. Sometimes drastic situations call for drastic measures. I am sure that my likeability did not rise on the scale, but it was the last time we had to address that issue. By the way, that young man went on to do a ton of outreaches for us later on that helped lead many to Christ. Was he ever perfect or likely to become a poster child for what a Christian should "look" like? I am thinking not. But, he became a powerful example of what God can do when people get out of the way and let God take control.

Despite constant opposition, resistance, and extreme religiosity we just kept pushing on. The senior pastor supported us at the time and he himself would oftentimes stand up to the board and assist in putting things in perspective for them. Be that as it may, he was undoubtedly limited sometimes. He had to proceed carefully in trying to balance building a relationship with the board and avoiding offending them against speaking out when things were not in line with Christian principles or behaviors. He knew that it was going to be a slow and arduous task of getting this church (let alone the board) on track. So, he oftentimes felt that he had to compromise or give in to the board even if it was blatantly obvious that they were being hyper-religious or controlling. He had specifically asked us to come onboard to help him knowing that we would be outspoken when biblical precedent called for it and that we could handle or even ignore most of the backlash while pushing forward. We could certainly handle a lot, yet we also knew that ministering in an environment like this is extremely taxing and it will ultimately wear you down. We were not sure if or when things would change so we just tried to enjoy all the good things that were happening in between episodes.

There was plenty to enjoy as far as ministry went. Now that the youth group was growing exponentially and spiritually, we could start introducing them to outreaches and evangelism. We knew we would need the youth because most of the adults were not all that interested or motivated to go out into the communities. There were some housing projects nearby, so we thought that we would start them out with reaching out to those needy folks first before tackling any major outreaches or youth prison ministries. The youth were doing great and really soaking things in. They liked reaching out to people, helping to provide to the needy and some of them were even developing some courage and boldness towards sharing the gospel. We thought things were going great but once again there was opposition. The board and some church members were concerned about their youth going into the projects as well as the influx of new visitors that had been invited to church that they considered less than desirable. Kind of a double whammy. They did not want to necessarily be the ones to go out into the community, but they also did not necessarily want them coming into the church either. What do you do? Incredible dilemma, right?

The senior pastor ultimately felt that he needed to start addressing some of the underlying religious issues and attitudes from the pulpit. Not solely to take the heat off us as the issues went well beyond just the areas of youth and evangelism ministries, yet they were certainly a big part of their target. Everything did not change overnight but it did seem to help some. I did not think much of it at the time, but his wife often intervened and wanted him to temper his exhorting or push back. She felt that we needed to have a softer approach with more patience and sensitivity toward the board and their religious friends, but we had already employed that approach for a very long time, and it was not working. And, the magnitude or severity of some of the issues as well as the unbiblical underlayment called for a quicker wake-up call if the church were to survive. Even if it meant potentially offending a few. We did not realize at the time that her motivation and perspectives were largely coming from her relationship and dialog with some of the board member's wives. Thankfully, he did not back off too much. There was still a lot of opposition and resistance but some of it was starting to diminish a bit. That was a welcome relief.

Many people in the "general congregation" and particularly new visitors were at least open to change and embracing a more evangelistic and open-armed atmosphere. And, more of the adults were stepping up to help volunteer and support the youth as well as outreach opportunities. We were able to start introducing them to a variety of different ministry opportunities like community outreaches, prison outreaches and even an inner-city mission trip to East St. Louis. The mission trip was not a popular decision since we cancelled their annually scheduled trip to the Bahama's. They had always gone on a mission trip to the Bahamas which unfortunately resembled more of a vacation than a mission trip when you looked at all the past photos.

I am not suggesting that the Bahamas does not need assistance or the gospel message, but I do know that if a mission trip is really comfy and you do not have to deal with any inconvenience or challenges that will get you out of your comfort zone then you are likely to not be nearly as effective as you could be. They had been going there for so long that it seemed as ordinary as doing church at home. So, when I conveyed to them that God wanted us to go to the inner city instead, it was definitely a shock to their comfort zones. I do not think I need to express to you at this point of the chapter how the board felt about it. Many of the adults that were initially scheduled to go on the trip backed out of going since it was not the Bahama's. Nonetheless, we pulled it off and those that went would come to admit later on that it was the best experience they had ever been involved with.

People always told me that the area where this church was located at was a tough one to minister in. But I found it to be tougher inside the church than it was on the outside. Although, things had at least improved in the church to the point that we were able to grow (and enjoy) what was happening with the youth and with outreaches. Despite all the opposition and resistance, we had come a long way and it was awesome to see what God had done with the young people. They were a much easier audience than some of their parents. Many of them were growing spiritually and getting out of the shells they had been living in for God knows how long. There was much to look back on and identify the progress that was made. Yet, we still had a way to go to try and rid the church of their dependency upon religion and religious practices or tendencies.

Board meetings were still an opportunity for some to snidely mock the good things happening, but it was at least tolerable, and I largely ignored it. Their attitudes and critical remarks were not surprising as very few of them ever participated in any of the outreaches, witnessing or youth events. On one hand I would like to say that we did not need them; but on the other hand, it is important and key for the leadership to visibly be involved.

We had experienced that blessing of support in other places we had been, and it goes a long way in building up your other volunteers. Because of the minimal support, I can confidently say that although we were experiencing success in many areas it was not nearly as powerful or as impressive as it could have been with positive leadership and involvement. And obviously in some ways it was a barrier. As they often say with most major changes "it will get worse before it gets better." We were about to find out how much worse.

One thing I guess that I did not anticipate was the senior pastor's wife becoming part of the controlling environment. She had become best friends with two of the most controlling board members wives. Women that she had talked about in a negative way in the beginning. That would be okay if she were merely trying to make amends for her past thoughts and comments about them, but she was actually taking on their same behaviors. It was hypocritical then to say the least. My wife had always felt like she was a bit possessive or controlling at times even when we all ministered together years ago, so I do not know if it was by design and she sought them out or it was just happenstance. However, it became a very visible clique. And, it did not make things any easier for us now.

She did not like that we had this new separate facility for the youth, despite that we worked hard to create it from an unused and cast aside storage place. The building which no one had ever taken the time or interest to change before. Let alone cleaning it up and getting rid of all the unneeded junk. Now that it was completely redesigned; her and the other wives suddenly wanted the space for their women's ministry area. As you might imagine that created some tension and problems. The senior pastor convinced us to compromise and resolve the issue by adding some big curtains or drapes on the walls that could hide all the youth decorations when prepping it for her events. And we now had to schedule or reschedule our activities around any events they planned. It is not unusual to have to share church facilities, but sharing was a bit of a stretch here because it really was not sharing. It seemed like they were all of a sudden "allowing" us to use the space occasionally. We were suddenly forced to also change or get rid of many of the decorations and items that they felt detracted from their purpose. And any change to scheduling would always demand that we check with them and change our activities no matter how long that it had been scheduled in advance.

Suddenly and unexpectedly she started becoming more vocal and critical of anything we organized. Particularly, if it was a successful event. Maybe it was always there, and we just did not know or hear about it. She joined in with the resistant crowd by vocally downplaying or criticizing ministries like our outreaches, prison, and youth detention ministries. Even our neighborhood witnessing that was either bringing in visitors or leading to new salvation commitments was subject to disparagement. Her criticisms typically involved comments about how they should have been done differently or better shall I say. Now I am open to suggestions or good ideas when it comes to evangelistic endeavors, but these comments were always criticisms and not mere suggestions or her volunteering to help in some way. She only liked to be part of the designing or decision-making...not actually helping out with any of it. Perhaps, she considered that to be the extent of her gifting, but even then it was not done in an edifying or encouraging manner. We were used to the opposition and criticism from the board; however, we were not used to receiving it from other staff members. Particularly, someone who had been around our outreaches and evangelistic events in the past and could not help but see the lives that were being changed and impacted.

All of a sudden, a new process was being implemented by her that required us to run practically everything through her as she was taking over "administration" of the church. Anything that we needed for our areas of ministry regardless of the cost had to be reviewed by her. She would then scrutinize its value and most likely scale it down or disprove of it altogether. If anything had to do with the poor or less fortunate that we were reaching out to then we needed to use less money or expense rather than do things in excellence as if they deserved less than the more affluent areas. Even petty cash or expense account items became such an issue that we just ended up paying for most things out of our own pockets. The change in her behavior took on the same persona as some of those that we had endured for so long already.

Sometimes it did not even matter if it was a church expense or not as we unexpectedly found out. My wife had taken it upon herself to decorate my office. Much like the renovation of the youth area, my wife used her own money for it and her own time to make it happen. Personally, I did not care as I know she likes to do things for the church out of the goodness of her heart and does a great job with adding some finer touches. If it were left to me, I probably would not have done much with it. But, she did an extraordinary job! Maybe too extraordinary given that the redecorating created a huge problem with the senior pastor's wife. Apparently, she perceived that I had a better office than she did. We might not have even known that it was an issue if it was not for the senior pastor coming to us and letting us know how upset she was. And you could tell by her more intense than usual snobbish behavior that something was awry. He tried to be gracious and just asked if we could ask first before decorating anything and run any plans by his wife first for her approval. Yes, even my own office. We knew in talking with him that just leaving it as is would most likely only continue to cause problems with her, so we ended up just stripping things down to the way it was before the decorating. It was a bit mind-blowing to me that something as trivial as decorating your office could be become such a major issue.

I do not think it would have mattered whether we left the re-decorated office the way it was or removed as much as possible. It would have undoubtedly been a problem either way as the issues obviously went beyond merely decorating my office. My wife also believed that she was increasingly jealous of my development as a preacher. I did not see myself as a threat as I knew my role and the specific ministries we oversaw and did not feel like I ever over-stepped any boundaries. I only preached in front of the whole congregation when asked to and never asked for more opportunities than I was given. Besides, we had our hands full with ministry and I got plenty of preaching opportunities with the weekly youth services or on our outreaches. I guess some of it had to do with the results we were seeing, but those belonged to God and the church anyway. Not to me. I always considered us to be a "team" working for the Lord. It should not matter who "gets credit" for it. I had not considered the potential that she was actively trying to minimize my opportunities and increase her husband's opportunities because it was usually under the guise that it was something the senior pastor should be doing or be in charge of. My wife could see it, but I really had not noticed. That is until the interference started to creep into my weekly preaching at the youth services or at our outreaches. I guess it became much clearer to me when we left for the inner-city mission trip to East St. Louis.

We had organized a weeklong mission trip in partnering with a great outreach ministry that was well-known for arranging inner city mission trips with churches. We had partnered with them before while serving at the prior church several years prior. Inner city St. Louis is a tremendous eye-opening and life changing opportunity for mission teams. We took a team with us while the senior pastor and his wife stayed back home. However, they decided to show up unannounced on the last two days of the trip right before a giant outreach that we had planned. They said that they came to help, but it was questionable as to what "help" meant when she clearly cherry picked which events to participate in and insisted on making changes to her liking.

Ironically, the chosen events were not the ones outdoors in the ninety-degree plus heat or the door to door witnessing in the projects. She decided to massively change the schedule of the big outreach event so that they were now the highlight and in control of the services and preparations that we had organized for the weekend. Even taking charge of our scheduled team meetings. We would have loved for them to come down and join us or help us serve the community, but it was rather obvious that this was more like taking over the reins completely. I cannot recall in any of our past outreaches ever having anyone else come to the outreach and try to take over like that. Nonetheless, we took a humble if not submissive approach and tried to accommodate all the changes as much as we could.

As tough as it was for the previous years of dealing with the board; this was a much more difficult and delicate situation. The senior pastor was a friend of mine that I served under and alongside for years. We had done so much ministry together. Pastoring, evangelizing, praying, witnessing, outreaching, and mission trips. I never felt like his wife just totally adored my wife and I, but I never felt unwanted or despised by her either. I just attributed most of the awkwardness and distance to her personality and maybe being a bit more of an introvert than him and I were. Although I had seen others in the past end up changing over time because of a position of power we had not anticipated this happening to our pastor friends. I am positive my friend the senior pastor understood what was going on because we both talked about things somewhat transparently in our offices many times. But he was in a tough predicament. Unfortunately, so was my wife and I now!

Perhaps, the worst church offense that we experienced was not an out in the open or public offense. It was the discovery that she was involved in behind the scenes gossip about us and our kids. When you talk or gossip about other families and their kids it is akin to attacking that family. It is a most unpleasant and damaging church offense that goes deep for most people who are subjected to it. Many people in the church think that pastor's kids or PK's are privileged. Some probably are. Yet, many other pastor's kids are actually under greater scrutiny or attack as they are held to higher standard or expectation than other people's kids. Kids are kids and should be held to the same standard regardless of their parent's title or role in the church. I get the concepts surrounding leadership that you are out front and you want to present a "superior" image, but subjecting kids to a forced religious standard is not healthy or even right. Just look at how many PK's have left the church once they were old enough to do so.

We never considered our kids privileged and we certainly never considered them perfect. Apparently, ours did not meet her standard and somehow compelled her and the other wives to gossip about it. I am not going to go deep here into how we discovered it or how we handled it. I will just tell you that we were aware of several instances where our kids were falsely accused, judged, and talked about behind our backs. It was only after we finally left the church that we actually found out the extent of just how much. Apparently, it happened much more often and far longer than we were aware of. The incidences we did know about were bad enough as they were.

The controlling spirit and the treatment of my family finally became too much to bear. We endured as long as we could, but unfortunately it was not a good environment and one that seemed to get worse in some ways instead of getting better. We felt that it was time to leave. I thought that I would never see another church environment like we did up in Washington, but that experience was almost like a walk in the park compared to this one. The ministries were doing great, but the opposition, resistance and far-reaching control was overwhelming. The unwillingness by the leaders to follow biblical principles or treat others with Christian character made for an environment that seemingly jumped from one issue to the next.

The board members and high-profile church leaders had grown used to the ways that they did things and they were blind to some of its unbiblical approach and poor treatment of others. Although spiritual growth was evident in many areas, it was overran by the leadership's blind manipulation. The school still remained as the most important component of the church and it still utilized monies from the general fund. I believe their tendency to hold up that school like a golden idol was a huge contributor to their blindness over decision-making, ethics and a Holy Spirit led approach.

God's direction appeared to be whatever they thought it should be because scriptural reference or precedence was often easily dismissed. The only times there was joy and peace were when we were able to conduct ministry but there was a heavy price to pay for those dividends.

I never fully realized the cost until well after the day that we left the church. It had exhausted us physically, mentally, emotionally, and spiritually over time. My family had sacrificed and endured a lot. I actually worked a midnight shift job while pastoring there because the salary at the church was not enough to support my family, although we ministered full-time and then some. That was okay because we loved ministry and we were somewhat used to a bi-vocational approach. In the evangelical churches that I ministered in and the denomination I was a part of; it was pretty typical for associate pastors (and sometimes even senior pastors) having to have a secular job while a church was starting out or growing. But it was physically exhausting, and the sacrifice oftentimes came at the expense of personal time with your family. When you are in environments like this you are compelled to look back and wonder if all the church hurt and sacrifice was worth it. Did God expect us to keep on serving and infinitely endure abuse and maltreatment from the very body we were trying to bless? At what point is enough really enough? I do not know where it is for others, but we had reached our point.

Although I knew we were drained spiritually and emotionally, I would not really know what it had cost us until well after we left. I really had no idea of the extent of the damage incurred by all the church offenses. Baggage that I would carry deep inside of me for a long period of time. And, now I had a cumulative inventory of church wounds because those that we had suffered up in

Washington that were hidden deep inside would also now rise to the surface and compound the severity of the overall damage. Sure, we had the outside look of some of that weariness and damage but much of it had been hidden and stored away just so we could function half-way normally. The wounds would unknowingly continue to fester deep inside of me only to rear its ugly presence in the form of resentment and pride down the road. That resentment and pride would ultimately cause unfathomable consequences for myself, my family and future ministry.

*** Special note

As I close out these chapters on the challenges of ministry we faced and I think back to the good, the bad and the ugly times we experienced; I cannot help but be reminded of a famous quote by Charles Dickens in the book A Tale of Two Cities that seems to sum it up best as it pertains to the early years of ministry for us...

"It was the best of times, it was the worst of times, it was the age of wisdom, it was the age of foolishness, it was the epoch of belief, it was the epoch of incredulity."[6]

The quote amazingly and accurately illustrates the contrast we experienced in ministry up to this point. We enjoyed many years of great ministry opportunities and we endured many years of brutal reality. We experienced years of exciting times and we also experienced years of attack that we wondered if they would ever end. We had the blessing of watching people's spiritual lives change and we had the curse of constantly combatting religion and religious attitudes. We had the honor of leading many people to the Lord and we had the burden of seeing unbelievable abuses in the church. We had more fun than we can possibly remember, and we had more trials than anyone should have to bear while serving.

We had the pleasure of serving under great godly leaders and we had the pain of serving under controlling and abusive leaderships.

I do not necessarily fault the people involved for all our bad experiences or church hurts that we were subjected to. They had merely adopted religion in the same way that anyone else has when it comes to sin and the blindness that often accompanies it. Yes, you hope and pray that they come to a realization of their behaviors to stop further offenses or damage to the Church, but you also know that they are imperfect as people no matter what their role, title, degree of influence or spiritual maturity level. However, that does not make it any easier to digest or heal from those offenses.

I tried to give you just a general feel for the atmosphere and opposition that we faced in several of our assignments. I do not have enough space and you do not have enough time to read about all the offenses we were subjected to in those years. Likewise, there is not enough space to adequately list all the successes and joy we had in serving. Perhaps that is what helped to sustain us through all the years of healing and provided the hope of returning to ministry sometime in the future. I trust that you will have a good enough depiction of what it must have been like and a sufficient amount of detail to understand the origin of the church hurts that would contribute or lead to the spiritual cracks in my own character later on.

8
PRIDE GOES BEFORE DESTRUCTION

After coming to the decision that it was time to leave the church assignment we were at, we ended up returning to our prior church. The one that we were at where we had overseen the outreach ministries, jail and prison ministries and evangelism ministry. We withheld from doing any ministry right away because we were primarily just looking for a safe place to attend and heal. We knew that we were hurting and had incurred some emotional as well as spiritual damage from all the church offenses so we knew that it would not be wise to just jump into a new ministry without first trying to heal. We knew we had sustained some damage but had no idea how deep or damaging those wounds were. The leadership was aware to a certain degree of what we had experienced so they supported our idea to just attend service and enjoy God's presence until some healing could take place.

Even though I was starting to grasp an understanding about church wounds, I was not really sure how much damage had been done. You can have a false sense of healing when you are suddenly immersed in a different and non-threatening environment, so it was difficult to assess the short-term and the long-term effects. We seemed okay and we were able to regularly enjoy "church" without constant conflict or personal attacks, so I contemplated that perhaps it was not as bad as initially thought. An atmosphere that suddenly allows you to merely sit back and enjoy worship, encouraging words from the pulpit and some well-deserved rest can help you to quickly shift your focus from recent bad experiences or even nightmares.

But if you haven't thoroughly resolved those issues and asked God to help you forgive those who brought on the offenses, then you have merely tried to cover up those wounds much like you would cover a physical wound with a band aid. The wound is still there. Even if it is scabbed over; it will resurface every time the scab is picked. Yet, many if not most of us handle them this way. It seems to be much easier to just cover over it as you do not have to revisit the pain. I pray that you come to understand how deceiving this is. Particularly if you have been subject to church wounds yourself. The enemy of your soul wants you to cover over those existing wounds to the point that you somehow think you have healed and moved on. He knows that it can make you immediately incapacitated in ministry or it will at some point.

While attending church regularly we were also able to invest back into our family time. I was still working the midnight shift job that I had while pastoring in Iowa, but I was now able to switch to daytime hours to invite a little more sanity and normalcy into our homelife. I worked at a place that was a youth shelter and PMIC facility (Psychiatric Mental Institution for Children). That job still allowed me to invest in young people, but in a different way as these were kids taken out of their homes for abuse and mental health issues. In many ways I loved being able to work there as it allowed me to gain great experience in the area of mental health. This would prove to be valuable down the road, but it was not a very high paying job and since I was not receiving any support from the church anymore I was needing to look elsewhere.

In the meantime, I had also decided to go back to school. I had gone to a Bible school to get licensed as a minister, but that was more like a certification for ministry rather than a full degree. It was accredited as a college, so those Bible courses counted toward my degree, but I basically only had the equivalency of an associate degree. So, I enrolled in a reputable local Christian University with full graduate and undergraduate programs. I was seeking to get my bachelor's degree, but attending a Christian college would also further my Bible and ministry knowledge. I was still hungry to learn more about the Bible, theology, and evangelism so it was a blessing to have local access. I was not tired of the church or the things about God; just tired of the religiosity and the people that use it as a weapon.

The school was not a "spirit-filled" college per se, but they had been evolving into a more non-denominational atmosphere that now accepted charismatic applicants whereas they had not done so in the past. They had a strong Mennonite and Baptist past so they were still more on the conservative or traditional side of doctrines associated with the Holy Spirit and spiritual gifts. The administration and school leadership had been changing over the years to be more accepting or open to some differing perspectives and a freer style of worship. They still struggled with it in some ways as the school had long been absent of any raising of hands, contemporary Christian music or displays of excited emotion while singing. The majority of the students were still very reserved or reluctant to go much beyond just standing or softly singing during worship. Some school officials I knew were even covert or closet spirit-filled supporters. Regardless of their conservative approach, they were biblically sound and a legitimate opportunity to get a degree in Bible, theology, ministry, and even secular vocations. They were progressively opening their attitudes and policies to support a little bit more dynamic or charismatic personality. Ultimately, I would not only receive my bachelor's degree from them, but I did a lot of my graduate work in counseling and theology. It was a great opportunity to continue my studies while taking a break from ministry.

After a lengthy period of almost two years removed from ministry I was approached by a long-time friend and mentor that wanted to offer an unexpected opportunity for full-time ministry. It was a ministry that existed outside of the church as a Christian foster care and group homes organization. It had already operated in the Lincoln area about fifty miles away from home for many years. However, this opportunity would involve pioneering a new branch of the ministry in Omaha as they felt led to expand their operations. I would be the only person to start out and I would be responsible for the recruiting and development of staff, recruiting of foster parents, building relationships with the local churches and all the training required. Additionally, the position also provided tremendous evangelistic opportunities for those foster kids that would be placed under our organization. It was an unbelievable opportunity that would also pay me far more than I had been making and was enough to sufficiently support my family. The opportunity to build something from the ground up was exciting in itself, but even more so without the burden of worrying about financial support that I had been used to carrying.

While starting out I just worked from home since we did not have an office in the Omaha area yet and we really did not need one until things grew to that point. Although I worked from home, I was on the road in the local area a lot. Starting the organization meant meeting with church leaders and discussing opportunities to speak to their congregations to inspire or recruit individuals to become Christian foster care parents. The foster care organization knew that I had a large network of church leaders in the area because of all the outreaches and ministry we had done locally and figured it would become extremely valuable when it came to gaining access. They were right. I was able to get access to a lot of churches and share about the program while recruiting new potential foster parents that could provide a Christian home and atmosphere for the youth. It might have taken a lot longer to pioneer or establish a new location if we had not been given an open door in many of the places. Sometimes they could offer only quick announcements and sign-ups after service and other times I was able to preach and inspire them to consider serving in this ministry. Either way we were developing at an unbelievable pace.

Initially, I thought it would be a slower process than it turned out to be regardless of my extensive network. My expertise in mental health and working with youth in a variety of dispositions (including behind prison bars) was proving to be an asset in nearly every aspect. It was useful in areas like training, supporting, and counseling new foster parents, interventions, relationships with the State and relationships with the foster kids themselves. The program was growing so fast and beyond expectations it was sometimes difficult to manage it all or keep up. We continuously added and trained new foster parents and the State was starting to place more and more kids in our homes. At the beginning of the growth spurt we added a new staff member about every 6 – 8 months and in less than 2 years we had increased the staff to 5 staff members. It was exciting growth to be sure, yet it became a very taxing responsibility.

If you are not familiar with how challenging it is to work with State government agencies, I can tell you that it is very difficult. Burnout is very common within their own ranks and anyone in the social services arena. In addition to the "red tape" or bureaucracy that you constantly had to work through; you were the in between entity or liaison for state workers, the judicial system, foster parents, biological parents, and the kids themselves. You could not possibly make all of them happy all the time no matter how hard you worked or how much progress was being made with the kids. Someone always had a complaint or criticism for how services were provided. You were pretty much subject to always being the bad guy or the fall guy for at least one of them to place all blame upon.

Being a "Christian" foster care program and trying to work with the government did not make it any easier. Growing the program would have seemed demanding all by itself. Many times, I had to fill any gaps that came up including even having some kids stay in our home. Occasionally, during emergencies or when there were no other options, we might have to take someone in for a little while until we could find a placement. My wife was tremendously gracious in opening our home on those occasions, but it did put a strain on the household at times. Oftentimes, she did not have time to prepare and we had our young daughter living at home who's safety and well-being we needed to consider as well. I probably was putting in anywhere from 60 to 80 hours per week. Eventually it was taking a toll on me. Not just physically, but other areas of my life were starting to show some effect.

The ministry was growing phenomenally fast in such a short period of time; so I would try to justify with my wife that all the investment of my time and energy was worth it and things would eventually slow down and level out at some point. Even though there were more staff members, I was still overseeing the development of the program, still doing most of the training and still doing the recruiting or speaking at churches. I did not mind the speaking because it still gave me opportunities to preach a lot of the time. But that takes preparation, investment and of course time of which I had very little of to begin with. In addition to those obligations, I had been asked more and more to simply come and preach at some churches. It was difficult to say no, and I seldom did. I was recognized as a good preacher with a lot of experience in teaching, preaching and evangelism so occasionally leaders would reach out and invite me to speak aside from the Christian foster care element. I was just not conscious of the toxic mixture of all the activities that were overloading me because I thrived on being able to accomplish them all. The more I was being fed about how good I was the closer I got to self-destruction as I pushed harder and harder to achieve even more success.

I did not clearly see what was happening to me as I worked hard to try and achieve success. Though my wife tried to caution me many times. Yet, I continued to push on and avoid the thought of giving up anything as I felt that I could still manage it all. I would have been too proud to admit that I could not handle everything considering all that I had been able to endure in the past and the success that was now being achieved. Regrettably, even though I was experiencing success in developing the program and my opportunities to preach on the side kept increasing, I was not seeing the effect that it was having on my character, marriage, or home life.

I was blind to some underlying issues that went beyond my drive to succeed and they were contributing to making things an even bigger problem.

First, I still had not realized the damage that was done from all the unresolved church hurts. If you would have asked me back then I would have assumed or thought that they were all taken care of and I had moved on. They did not appear to be front and center in my life, so I basically ignored any thought that there could still be any residue or effects from the past wounds. The success of building a growing ministry from essentially nothing and newly found opportunities to preach on the side seemed like evidence towards confirming that I had healed over time.

If discussion ever came up about the past church hurts, I even somewhat laughed it off and dismissed the possibility that any lasting impact remained. However, that was more of an emotional façade because I knew that many of those offenses were never resolved in my spirit or with God. The truth was that I had not forgiven many people from the last church including some of the board members, their wives the senior pastor's wife and even my friend the senior pastor. Nor had I totally forgiven some of those that wounded us at the church up in Washington years ago. Despite my perceptions or contentions that the offenses no longer "bothered" me. Just because I was able to function normally, and a huge amount of time had passed since we left there; it was not an accurate indicator of what I really felt about it all. The enemy deceives you into thinking merely because you have seemingly moved on that all is well. All was not well.

The emotions of anger, bitterness and hurt had taken a deep foothold inside of me. It was so deep that it was well hidden from any outside noticeability other than the impact it was having on my character and personal life that most people beyond my wife could not see because I hid it so well. I did not think that I was angry or bitter, so I merely did not act like it. Hurt? Yes, but I convinced myself that probably everyone gets hurt in the church so I could learn to deal with that. Besides I had convinced myself that since I was in a new full-time ministry that not only treated me with great respect and that was also showing great success—-because of what "I" was building——that it was even more proof that the wounds no longer affected me.

The problem is not solely or even primarily with the emotions of anger and bitterness. It is with what they will develop into. Anger and bitterness are human emotions so practically everyone experiences them to varying degrees. Even God and Jesus are talked about as being angry in the Bible although it was righteous anger which is a different exhibition of anger. If left unaddressed anger and bitterness will give rise to resentment and pride. This had been developing inside me for years now and just kept getting worse as it fed upon the successes in ministry that I was experiencing. The real problem was not how much effort and time that I was putting into the ministry or into new preaching opportunities but rather their contribution as a catalyst for developing pride and resentment out of the anger and bitterness from unresolved church offenses. The more success and opportunities that I was getting; the more prideful and resentful I was getting. The more that people appreciated and praised my abilities; the more that my ego and inner pride was growing. The more my wife raised concern; the deeper I went into denial.

I did not think I was prideful because I could still outwardly act humble. But there was no doubt that pride was increasing inside of me and encouraging resentment towards all those who had any part of the poor treatment that my family and I had undergone while pastoring at our last church. Pride fed off resentment and resentment helped to fuel more pride. If you think that there is an easy remedy for identifying this... there is not. I think in most cases you are blind to it as it grows unless you are fortunate enough to discover it before it gets out of hand. I was not.

My wife had always been my protector and voice of accountability. And for the most part I almost always followed her lead or warnings in this area. As a pastor or in any ministry your wife can always see things in you and in others that you do not see. That is another reason why God calls both of you into the ministry as a team even if one is the more active partner. This insightfulness is especially true if you happen to have a wife like mine who was not only insightful but acutely listened to the voice of the Holy Spirit. She warned me about my growing arrogance and the increasingly poor treatment of her and my family. Yet, I growingly dismissed it and even started blaming her for our problems. I only saw this much later after already causing much damage to our marriage. It is something that I have had to live with along with the accompanying sadness and remorse after finally realizing how badly I treated her. It was totally undeserved and notably so when you consider that all she was doing was trying to help and convey what the Holy Spirit was showing her. This is one of the many important reasons that the damage of church offenses are so critically important for me to share with you in hopes that you will resolve yours long before you ever reach the point that I did.

More and more holes started to surface in my character. I grew up in ministry learning about the importance of establishing "fences." I took them seriously and adopted or embraced them as essential to surviving in ministry. Fences are principles that you put in place and adhere to in order to guard your honor, integrity, ministry, and marriage. They primarily are in reference to behaviors around females other than your wife (although you can have them in other areas.) They help you to purposely avoid areas or scenarios that could get you into fast trouble with women. Some of them are simple rules like avoiding hugs while ministering to women. Especially when they are distraught or emotional. Other fences like giving women or young girls rides home all by yourself (including babysitters) may seem like a no brainer but it is probably one of the most frequently dismissed or ignored by males. There is almost an ignorant attitude about it and yet, the number of inappropriate instances still happening today is astonishingly high. Other areas of concern that demand some type of fence or protection include scheduling luncheon appointments with women all alone (even if it is business or church related), and even closed-door counseling sessions that the secular world does not seem to think twice about.

The implementation and adherence to fences had always saved me in the past from more situations than you can imagine. It is not just yourself that you must worry about or how strong you personally are to resist temptations or thoughts. You must also consider the intentions, emotions, or vulnerability of the other party. Every pastor or male serving in ministry is vulnerable or a potential target to this area and needs to be aware of it. It would serve you well if you are married to also have a wife that is aware of it and closely guarding you. That may still not stop you from abandoning those principles if you are in a dire spiritual state like I was, but it may stop you from ever getting there. You need to establish rules and behaviors that keep you from unexpected temptations, potential of a moral failure or even the possibility of an "alleged" impropriety.

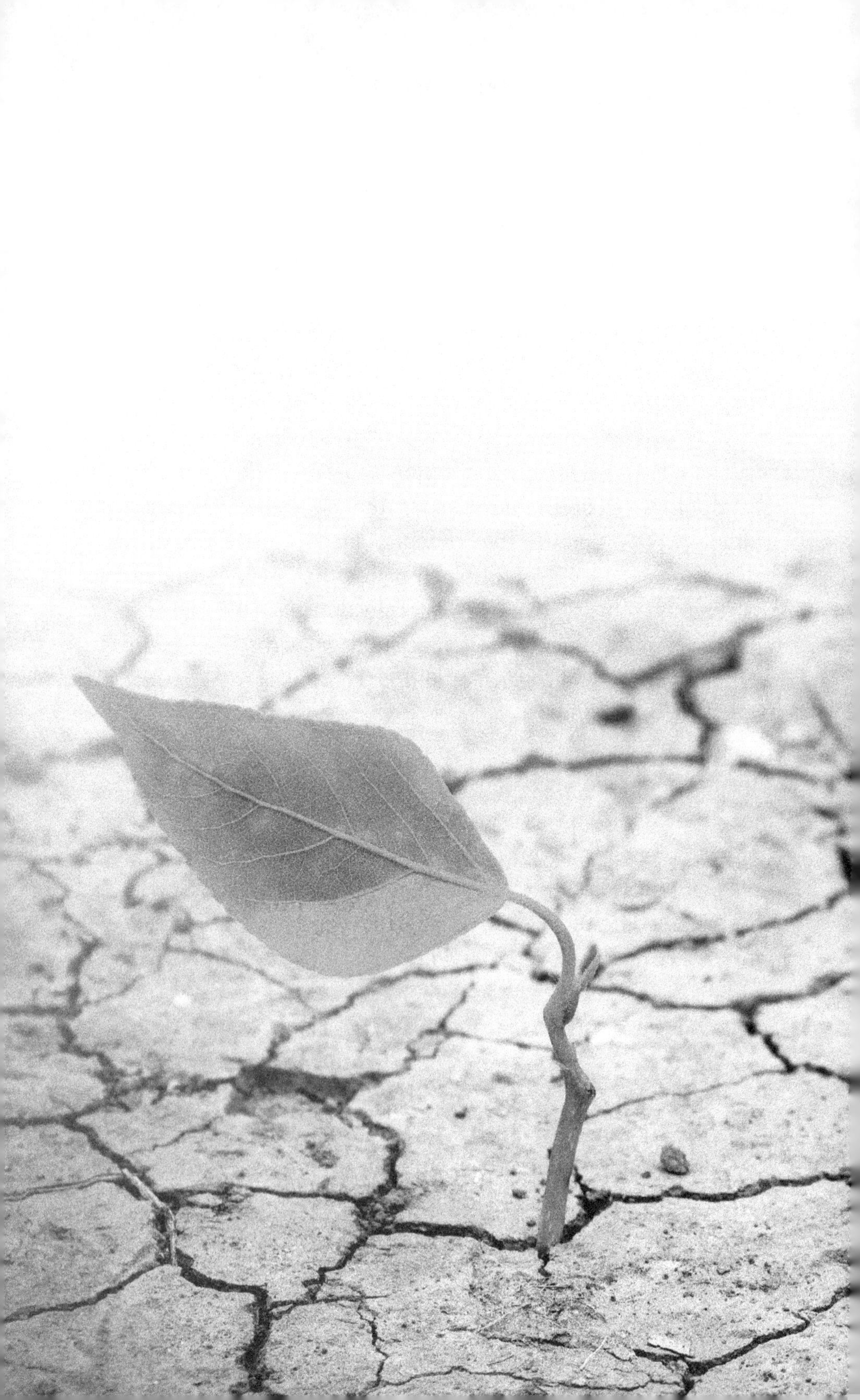

9

THE UNPARDONABLE SIN

Eventually the cracks in my character became gigantic holes. Large enough for a moral failure to seep in. I had a brief affair with one of the female staff members at the Christian foster care program and God exposed it. Note that I say brief here because it was, and I do not want your mind racing with speculation without knowing that. It is almost a natural reaction for people to instantly start speculating or imagining the details when they first hear the word "affair" or "sexual misconduct" without even knowing the story behind it. Society and the church both have trained us that way. Besides, I do not believe the damage is reduced or the offense is somehow more palatable regardless of whether it was a one-time thing or a long-lasting affair. The consequences that are life-long for me and particularly devastating at the onset are not subject to a sliding scale of punishment. Rest assured that using the word "brief" is not for the purpose of deflecting or trying to minimize the horrendous implications or severity of the issue. Those close to me including my wife know how full circle I came with what I did and took personal accountability for it.

God exposed the affair to my wife first who had suspected it with most assuredly the help of the Holy Spirit. She had been vigorously fighting for our marriage and had even straightforwardly asked me at times if I was having an affair. I of course denied it and would forcefully put the blame of our marital problems on her so as to take the focus off myself. The deflation of my character and reputation was in a huge disarray if not totally destroyed. The inattention I had given to the growing resentment and pride for several years had now led to sinful acts of deception, infidelity, denial, spousal abuse, selfish ambition and outright lying. It is mind boggling to what extent someone will go to deny covert behaviors. Even after they have been indisputably found out. People really look foolish when denying something that is blatantly obvious or exposed to everyone around them. I am sure that I was no exception and looked foolish trying to defend myself.

What most people do not understand however, is the complexity and spiritual implications of what all goes into a situation like this. I certainly did not, and I used to occasionally do marriage counseling as an associate pastor. Many other pastors that I have met with and discussed this with after my moral failure have little to no clue what all is typically involved. I am quite certain that no affair merely starts by someone waking up and deciding to go cheat on their spouse. Even those absent of any church or spiritual involvement in their lives whatsoever most likely have some type of build up to the act.

The unresolved anger and bitterness that I started with had evolved into pride and resentment. It then escalated beyond the deeply hidden emotional stage to start affecting me psychologically and at least some if not all areas of my character and spiritual life. It typically chips away at smaller areas of your character like mild deception or lying that you can initially get away with so as not to make you instantly aware of a growing problem. However, it eventually raises to an even greater level of personal destruction by gaining access to your spiritual core that shuts off a connection between you and the Holy Spirit. At least temporarily. The timeline may differ for individuals, but I believe that essentially it generally follows the same process unless they are fortunate enough to identify it early on and avoid some of the disastrous consequences.

I had become so insensitive to the Holy Spirit that all my actions and behaviors seemed to be easily justified. I had come to believe that my lies and perceptions reflected reality instead of deception. Many of the things that I am telling you now were not so apparent or visible to me back then. I can only tell you now of what it was like after looking back on it and taking years to break it down. The reason I could not have identified all of this for you back then is because there is a bewitching component to it. When you reach the level that you have shut off access to the Holy Spirit or have stopped listening to Him; then you have no choice but to listen to other voices. Your own and of course any others that you might entertain including the enemy.

I am quite sure that many of you will either not know what I mean by bewitching or be tempted to think that I am just looking for a way out of being personally accountable. I say that because many family members and friends have scoffed at that idea over the years thinking it is too bizarre of an explanation or a convenient excuse. I can assure you that is not the case. I have endured more hardship than you can possibly fathom and especially if you have not personally experienced something like this. I pray that you have not. I believe one of the main reasons for divorce in situations like this is because someone did not want to take accountability for their actions. Divorce seems like a more appealing and much more painless route to take because you can continue to live in a state of denial for years. Quite frankly, coming to grips with all that I had done and all the damage I had done to those I love was not for the convenient sake of minimizing consequences in my life. I have endured consequences that you probably have no idea about and I know the pain and agony of them quite well.

My actions would unleash a torrent of consequences and chain of events that caused destruction in nearly every part of my life. I would lose my job, lose our home, lose many of our personal belongings that had to be sold, lose many of my best friends, lose my favorite dog of all time and instantly be out of ministry. Merely describing it as financial ruin and some personal losses would be a huge understatement. However, even more important was the realization that I was on the verge of losing my wife and I had no control over that no matter how sorry I might be. I caused hurt and pain for my wife, my kids, and close friends that they did not ask for nor did they deserve. I no doubt also had a part in causing the same potential damage to the other party's family and home life. I lost the trust and respect of so many people who had believed in me and supported me in ministry for many years.

For a long time, it almost felt as if I had lost everything. Do you honestly think if I really understood what the consequences would be like... that I would have been willing to easily give all that up? The bewitching component does not allow you to use any foresight and really see the consequences or the potential pain and damage that will happen. If you are someone who has tragically gone through a situation like this and you were the unfortunate recipient of your spouse's infidelity and they have failed to take responsibility for it or they have seemingly escaped major consequence; I can assure that was not my case. Many consequences like just the sheer remembrance of your failure will stary with you for the rest of your life. Sure... God, my wife, my kids, and others have forgiven me, but I do have to live with the reality of remembering the things I have done in my life and the damage that they caused. I will forever be forced to be extraordinarily conscientious about doing all I can to avoid even the slightest bit of impropriety or speculation. Perhaps, that is not such a bad repercussion in light of its influential awareness that can help to any kind of future failure.

Even after all these years and all the forgiveness, it is not an easy thing to just openly share. Just stop and think about some of the hidden things in your life that you enjoy the luxury of no one else or very few knowing about and how you might feel if it were made public. I have made myself extremely vulnerable by sharing things about my life that you would have otherwise never known. I have chosen to do this (with God's leading and grace) for the purpose of exposing the truths and trying to help you avoid the potential devastation if you or someone else is headed down this path. If you think that it cannot happen to you then you are sorely mistaken. I had several pastor friends after my fall sit and tell me about their great plans for protecting themselves and how their fences protected them. I had fences. Plenty of them and a wife sensitive to the Holy Spirit to watch out for me. I cautioned them in their unseen arrogance back then. Sadly, but almost expectedly, none of them are serving in ministry today and they are all divorced. Do not make the same ignorant and prideful mistake of patting yourself on the back because you happen to have fences or principles.

Let me go back to the bewitching component that I mentioned to you. It may be difficult for some of you to understand if you have not experienced it or "identified" it in the past. It was what kept me from the necessary conviction to change paths and turn back from the destruction that lay ahead. It also kept me from immediately admitting my wrong doings and taking ownership of my immoral actions. When I was found out I did not instantly take full responsibility or consideration for all my behaviors. I found myself taking on a worldly perspective as if my wife and maybe others were partly responsible and somehow drove me to my actions. I was not even grasping the gravity of the impending consequences. It took somewhere between a week or two after I had already moved out of our home before the Holy Spirit was able to make any breakthrough in my thought processes or successfully convict me of my sins. My daughter confirmed that the opening of my eyes took only about two weeks or less, but either way it seemed like an eternity. When it finally happened, it was as if scales had been literally removed from my eyes to see all that I had done and caused. The horror and sudden realization of it all was practically unbearable.

My marriage was in deep jeopardy as my wife had already seen a lawyer. The prompting by her family members and others led to that advisement in order to immediately protect her interests. Although she was somewhat reluctant to do so. I finally understood the deeper illustration of what it meant in the Book of Genesis when God brings two together and makes them one. I had a void in my spirit and in my heart like I have never experienced. It was extremely painful and burdensome. It went way beyond what some might try to classify as guilt or physiological side effects. And NO...it was not just the fear or prospect of losing my wife. It is a much deeper and more real spiritual experience than mere thought or contemplation. It is almost as if your body is an empty shell. Even as a pastor or evangelist I never fully understood that meaning until that moment. I believe that is why denial is such an appealing tool for many people going through divorce, so they will not experience that spiritual reality or other consequences and possibly change their mind about admitting to their sin. Believe me when I tell you that bewitching is very real regardless of how bizarre it might sound to you.

The chain of events after the discovery of my infidelity were some of the most soul scarring moments of my life. They far exceeded the abuse and neglect that I experienced while growing up in a dysfunctional home. To simply say they were unpleasant, distressing, miserable or even horrid would be an injustice. The first task that I did was to move out immediately. It seemed like the expected thing to do. Remember that I still had scales on my eyes that prevented me from even acknowledging the wrongdoing or discussing it with my wife before moving out. I am not sure that she would have even wanted me there if I had asked her, but I never afforded her that opportunity. I reached out to a friend that I had done outreaches and ministry with for years and he and his wife graciously allowed me to move into their unfinished basement. I was grateful as I really did not have any other place to go.

I immediately resigned from my position of ministry and I also submitted my resignation for my license to the local officials of my denomination. I am not sure why I felt it was so imminent to immediately resign my ministerial license, but I am thinking that the spiritual implications where the enemy could claim victory for disabling my ministry had something to do with it. I spent the next week or so trying to figure out how to move forward. My spiritual state was still a mixture of defiance and justification, so I was looking at things from a worldly perspective. I was not even all that concerned about ministry or the far-reaching implications yet.

I had talked to my son and daughter who were old enough to understand basically what was happening and as you might imagine...they were not happy with me. My son was now in the military and my daughter was a junior in high school, so they indeed understood some of the implications but there were many aspects that they did not yet grasp. They did not understand my seemingly unapologetic attitude that was part of the bewitching component. They were not used to that level of arrogance and defiance from me in the past. I had no idea what I would do for a job now, but I had finished my bachelor's degree and was within a couple of months of completing my master's degree, so I don't remember being too concerned about it while under the spell of evilness. Of course, I still had the pride issue in my spirit so I am sure that I thought I could make whatever work.

At some point I finally had a reality check with the Holy Spirit and knew that I needed to go visit my pastor at a smaller church we had been attending lately. We had been attending and volunteering there since I went into full-time ministry. We had switched churches largely because I was afforded preaching and teaching opportunities there, but they had also grown to be great friends. They are the ones I mention in the acknowledgements. Great man and woman of God. If nothing else I knew that I needed to let him know as a friend what had transpired, although, I was sure that my wife had already made them aware of the situation. I met him at the church, and he was waiting in the sanctuary. Praying for me I imagine. I could not even get any words out for the longest time because things suddenly and "finally" came full circle, and a huge spirit of conviction was upon me. The scales had been removed from my eyes and the horror of it all was on full display for my conscience to face it all head on.

If you are thinking that it was just emotional manipulation to make me feel bad and finally get through to me; you would be gravely mistaken. He had not even said anything yet. And, keep in mind that I had plenty of opportunities to "get emotional" prior to this occasion. If an emotional atmosphere were all it took then I would have already lost it in discussions with my kids or where I was now staying because they were into Jesus big time. I was also surrounded by reminders of God and worship music playing all the time and that had not made a dent in my obstinate or unyielding attitude up to this point.

No, it was the presence of the Holy Spirit and a great friend with a pastor's heart that finally broke down the barrier. Just getting to this place was miraculous progress, but it meant that I now had to deal with reality. Much of the impending implications and consequences were somewhat blind to me up to this point. Now I was faced with "what do I do now?" It was tremendously humbling and overwhelming because I had "prided" myself on always having an answer or solution in the past and I had no clue as to what to do now. The fact of the matter was that things were totally out of my control now anyway.

My pastor friend counseled me that evening without it even seeming like a counseling session. He and his wife possess the delicate balance of embracing you with unconditional love but having the courage to speak truth to you as needed. Just as I had thought earlier, he and his wife had already met with my wife. He spoke straightforward with me and told me that my wife loved me deeply, but she was now deeply hurt as well. Not just ticked off or hurt a little bit; hurt deeply and a lot of damage had been done. As a matter of fact, he just did not know if we would make it through this. He poignantly advised me that I could not focus on that but rather that I need to just put my focus on Jesus and rely on God's will to be done even if the result were not to my liking. He knew that you can't just avoid all concern about your marriage, but if that was my focal point then it was on the wrong area because only God could repair the damage I had done and speak to her heart. And if there was one thing for sure...she loved and trusted God.

So, that is what I did. I was up at the church every single day to pray. He always was there at the church early and had the sanctuary open with soft music playing in the background. Because that is what he did everyday anyway. Then he would go on to tackle church business and leave me by myself until I was done. At first, I did not want him to leave but he knew I needed some alone time with God. The church was going through a renovation of sorts and since I was now unemployed, I spent most of my days working up there and helping to re-build. It was very timely you might say. Just the atmosphere alone was like a healing balm.

When I say like a healing balm; do not misunderstand and think that healing was taking on a rapid pace. I still did not know what the future held and if our marriage would even survive. My wife was meeting with them independently just as I was and attending church, but I had not even seen her face to face in weeks or months. I am not sure exactly as some of it is hard to recollect and purposely so. In the very early going of my prayer times up at the church I had made two requests of God. I asked him to save my marriage and I would find a way to come back and serve Him in ministry again someday and the other request was to purge as much from my mind as He possibly could. I knew I could not forget everything, but I wanted Him to help me forget as much as possible.

Down the road a bit later as part of her own healing process my wife wanted some details of the affair from me. I believe she was testing me for transparency at that stage so I would give her all that I could in trying to be 100% transparent, but sometimes I had to tell her that I could not remember. It was difficult for her to believe me that I honestly could not remember as I had become such a huge liar before the fall in ministry. Some of the lack of recollection was because of the bewitching element involved and the scales that had been over my eyes and mind. You simply do not see things or are able to recollect some things when you are under it and you also still do not see some things when removed from it because it was not reality that you were living under in the first place. God has helped me to erase a lot from my memory. As you can see by this chapter, He did not purge everything I would have liked him to, but He has done a lot. During the years it took for us to heal my wife would bring up things that I sincerely had no recollection of whatsoever.

After a while, our pastors were able to arrange a joint session with us and them at their house. Seemed safe enough and I was excited about us meeting. I am sure I jumped the gun thinking it was progress as it was put into brutal perspective relatively quickly for me. She not only let me have it (and understandably so) but it became very clear that we were still a long way off from even considering whether our marriage could be saved or not. Yet, it was extremely good to see her. She looked great but of course I could not tell her that. She really did not want to hear too much of me as I think she wanted me to hear more of her instead. She had heard enough from me in the past most likely. I did get a picture of the physical impact the stress can play on you as it was obvious that we were both losing a lot of weight. We were still apart and the only time we saw each other was at an occasional joint session or when I might drive by the house to try and catch just a glimpse of her and my daughter or to shovel the snow. That would scare the daylights out of her she told me later. It was heart-wrenching for me to think that my wife was afraid of me for some reason. I had never been violent towards her, but that was an illustration of just how much damage had been done to the trust and peace in her life. I am not sure how many weeks and months elapsed but eventually we reached a point where we went to service together. The healing process was happening; however, you may not have thought that for several years as we seemingly took one step forward and two steps back. Eventually, it would evolve into two steps forward and one step back.

In the meantime, the denomination that I was licensed under had rejected my resignation. I was a bit perplexed initially and not understanding their actions. They conveyed to me that proper protocol was to assemble a local committee of 3 or 4 pastors to meet with me to discuss the situation and then go from there. I agreed to meet with them without any idea as to why it was really necessary or what would it amount to in the future. When I met with them I was not too intimidated because I knew two of the members really well and had trusted them in the past. I had to share all the details that had led up to the moral failure and whatever I could offer them up to the current date. A stumbling point arose when I could not identify a concrete plan that I had for re-entering into ministry or commit immediately to their own rehabilitation plan that they had in place. I tried to convey to them that I was entirely focused on my marriage and re-engagement with my children. Those issues were still very much up in the air with no idea how everything would eventually pan out. My wife and I were still separated and although we were going through counseling it was obvious that any possibility of resolution was way off in the future and it was in God's hands with His timing if it even were to happen at all.

Apparently, the understanding of having to focus on my marriage for now was unacceptable as they believed you should be working on both at the same time and be able to afford some explanation or plan for re-entering into ministry. Thus, I was given notice later that because of my inability to provide specific details and timelines I was defrocked of my credentials. Even though I had tried to willingly resign my credentials months earlier; I was subject to having it publicly noted and published in their newsletter for all to see. Arguably, a type of public shaming. This was really disappointing and yet another huge church offense that I would have to overcome in the following years. I understand their intent to try and salvage an opportunity for someone to re-enter ministry; but they obviously had no understanding of how something like this impacts your life. Nor did they apparently understand the order of God, family and then church.

This is one of those church offenses that is left for you and God to settle because the reality of approaching their top leadership to have them consider changing their insensitive denominational process was simply not feasible at the time. It still may not be up for debate or consideration. I do not know if they have made changes to the way that they approach these matters, so all that I could do is ultimately forgive them and pray for them. My prayer is that they learn how to effectively minister to those in these situations and avoid unnecessarily putting someone else through the traumatic experience that I had to endure. There is no benefit to publicly shaming someone. I firmly believe that if they had just waited a while for God to heal us and be open to considering His timeline for accomplishing that; I most likely would have re-entered ministry a long time ago.

After months of separation and occasional joint counseling sessions my wife and I were able to start attending services together. This is very difficult to do because no matter how confidential your pastors are; word will somehow get out. Or, they will figure that something is up with your marriage and ministry just by the sudden changes that are visibly evident. In some cases, you know that they know and in other cases you at least think that they know by how they act towards you. It made it too difficult of an atmosphere for us to try and heal under. Our pastors totally understood this predicament and released us to go find a place to heal. We knew they would be praying for us and not just saying that they would and would welcome us back at any time that we felt we had healed sufficiently and felt led to return. We had no idea at the time that it would take over fifteen years before that time came.

It did not take us the entire fifteen years to heal sufficiently. It just took that long before "all" things had been resolved including past church offenses before we were ready to return to their church and finally be ready for a return to ministry.

In the meantime, we did have a lot of healing needing to take place and a lot of repair work to our relationship. I had lost the trust that my wife had in me and that would take a long time to regain. I made a promise to her that I would always fight no matter how difficult it was and periodically she would feel compelled to test that fight to see if I would give up. She also wanted me to hurt, so she would tell you today that she intentionally tested those waters by expressing doubt as to whether we could ever make it back or if the propagated cliché that your marriage "can be even better than it was" was all a hoax or fallacy. Not because of any ungodly or vicious motivations of her own; but rather because of the pain and psychological damage I had caused.

Additionally, we had to deal with "triggers" for years. Dates, anniversaries, familiar sites, memorabilia, or other items that would just ironically or coincidentally "pop up" to create some set back. Even totally unexpected instances like the mention of particular names or watching a movie where a reference ignites a memory could easily disrupt our progress and make it seem as if we had to start all over again. It got easier to manage or less volatile over the years and the incidences would get farther and farther in between each one to allow even more healing to take hold.

Hopefully, the explicit details provided in this book will also help someone going through this to understand what is going on. It takes quite a bit to get beyond the incidences and realize that they are not a mere coincidence. And, I am convinced that it is a typical if not standard process that anyone going through this has to face. The enemy is still involved, and convenient hurdles or reminders can rekindle thoughts or pick that scab that has not fully healed yet. Even when God does heal you; you will then still have to overcome the next stage of learning to live with those scars.

Although the horrendous consequences are primarily related to the relationship with your spouse and your relationship with

God; they certainly go well beyond that. And, religion will be right there to step in and make sure that you do not escape any of them. Another damaging consequence was with the relationship to my son and daughter. They were both angry with me although my daughter was more so hurt and angry than my son. Maybe it was gender related, age related or because he was away from home in the military, but it was more difficult with her.

Over time they were both able to deal with it as we appeared to be on the path towards restoration of our marriage, but I knew that they had not yet truly forgiven me. I cautioned both of them that they would sometime in the future be tempted to use it against me when it best served their interests, or they felt that they had no other weapon to use against me other than my personal shortcomings. That came to pass in later years where each of them within the confines of a disagreement angrily voiced that "at least they weren't like me or did the things that I did." It is the epitome of a religious self-righteousness that wants to compare severity of sins but when it is this close to home the anger and hurt are also in play. I understood where it was coming from and it was okay because I knew that I had caused the initial hurt. It did help them however, to ultimately forgive me and enjoy the relationships that we have today. Nonetheless, it is not something that is pleasant or that you want to experience as a parent when you have let them down and caused damage that will take a long time to heal from. Once again, if you think I have escaped consequence then you have no idea on how it feels to have your children be impacted in this way where they make it explicitly known to you.

Beyond my family, there were even more consequences for me to experience. I had not considered the impact that it would have on my friendships nor the responses I would receive from members of the Church body. Particularly the leaders. I lost perhaps my best friend in ministry that hired me for the foster care ministry. We talked for many months after the fall from ministry but then I approached him and let him know that I needed some time away from communicating with him because it was a bit painful for my wife at the time. He was somewhat of a representation of where everything took place and my wife even partially cast some of the blame on him during her time of pain. Aside from ministry, he had a strong mental health background so I thought he would understand the difficult process, yet he apparently took it personal and has not talked to me since. I have tried several times over the years to reach out to him, however he has not responded. I am saddened as I would love to have his forgiveness and friendship, but I do not know if it will ever be available again. A consequence that I apparently must accept and endure.

I have had more relationships within the church that came to an end than I can probably accurately recall. I have had pastor friends that immediately cut off all communication and abandoned our friendship or some of them that consciously limit their dialog now to just a cordial greeting. I have had elders and their wives whom I closely knew that would obviously and intentionally walk on the other side of the sanctuary from us or even avoid me altogether out in public. Even literally running away from you in a store as if you had the plague.

Then there were also those that clearly showed that they may even stand by you for a little while and then give up on you because they cannot handle the long wait for your healing to end. That is heartbreaking! They obviously do not have the same level of patience that God has. I have had some pastor friends give up on us during the healing process and be so bold as to tell me "to get over it" without them having a clue as to what's involved in the healing process or yielding to God and His timeline. You would think that they would somehow figure out that they must be wrong and are not hearing from the Holy Spirit when even their wife is appalled at them for saying things like that.

Additionally, I have sat through numerous insensitive if not ignorant messages from the pulpit about adultery. Yes, I like many others in the beginning was certainly prone to being overly sensitive at times; however, I am talking about long after I have healed. Those instances where they are clearly preaching from a limited knowledge at best and an approach that unequivocally categorizes infidelity as somehow being a worse sin. I can assure you that I know the difference between having a "perception" of being offended merely because I am still hurting versus being acutely aware of how infidelity is incompetently being addressed from the pulpit.

Now you know where the inspiration for the title of this chapter comes from. I titled this chapter this way because the Lord has shown me over the years how adultery is essentially the unpardonable sin in the Church. Not in God's eyes, but rather how those in the body including some leaders have succumbed to treating it differently than other sin and unfortunately treat the people coming out of it differently as well. Some of you may have been chomping at the bit to discover what was in this chapter or why I would include "the unpardonable sin" from the Bible in the book in the first place. Especially if you are the deep theologian type that likes to debate what "the unpardonable sin" actually is. I can tell you that I was involved in many discussions in several Bible schools and universities that dispute the meaning or interpretation of the unpardonable sin. Most have resolved it to mean some type of blasphemy against God or the Holy Spirit without fully being able to define the specific offense or offenses. However, almost all positions would at least agree that it is an offense so egregious that goes beyond the pale of most if not all other sins. That is why I use it as somewhat of a metaphor here to label how many in the church view or treat adultery. You may still feel inclined to think otherwise but that would most likely be because you have not had to experience anything like this.

On the surface you may not think that you treat adultery any differently than other sins or treat people differently whom you know were involved in infidelity; yet, I wonder how often you have truly examined yourself and sincerely asked that question. If you are not closely associated with it in some way it is unlikely that you think about it much. Why would you? You may even subconsciously avoid digging too deep into issues like that in the Bible and just be content with speaking about it from what little knowledge or ministerial background that you might have.

Many of you can probably easily quote Bible verses that point out that "all have sinned" or how all sin is equal in God's eyes but how many would admit that they may have a tendency to categorize or weigh certain sins? Out of the choices between lying, cheating, stealing, cheating on your taxes, murder, adultery, drug abuse, prostitution, gossiping, porn, greed, pride or even actions out of anger: Which one is worse? Or even better yet…… what about some other lesser known possibilities like lack of empathy, absence of grace or mercy, unforgiveness, favoritism, judging others, deception, or selfishness?

Are only the "Thou shalt not's" that are written in the Ten Commandments the big sins to focus on or worry about?

What is really sad is when the secular world or those outside the church seem to do a better job with forgiveness or at least moving on from affairs that become public knowledge than some people inside the church. I would certainly agree that the world is perhaps a bit too forgiving or complacent with the issue but the difference between the world and the church when it comes to judgement or judging others is surely noticeable. Yes, people make bad choices, mistakes and decisions that are worthy of consequence, but it should not be an opportunity for the church to add to those consequences. They should be involved in the restoration portion rather than the abandonment role.

Some sins do seemingly carry greater consequence regardless of whether we categorize them or not. But that is by God's design and not by human distinction. Certain sins like adultery, abortion and murder will undoubtedly carry consequences that will last a long time, if not a lifetime. I will be the first to tell you that. They produce emotional, spiritual, and even sometimes physical scars. At the very least you will be subtlety reminded of the load that you bear because of a scar or a lasting effect even after God forgives you and restores you. But, should the church be inflicting further wounds upon you because of their religious attitudes and failure to represent God's entire character? I am thinking God would say a resounding "no."

Special note for pastors and leaders that are not qualified to speak on adultery***

Acts of infidelity, adultery, affairs or whatever you want to call them continue to be an "unpardonable sin" for many people in the body of Christ. I know this to be true because I continue to see how others going through it have been treated. I have witnessed many incidences in the years since I went through it and was restored, so I know that it is not over-sensitivity on my part. And, those incidences are only the situations that I do happen to know about.

Pastors, church leaders and other believers need to learn how to deal with this issue more appropriately in order to expedite healing in those going through it instead of their past practice of hindering it. It has bad enough consequences in and of itself without the aid of further pain coming from the Church body. All sin is bad in God's eyes and He does not categorize or establish levels of sin like we have the tendency to do.

It does not have anything to do with watering down the severity of the transgression but rather avoiding the potential of wrongly contributing to someone's consequences. God is in control of the consequences and He does not need our reminders or opinions on how a sinner should be dealt with. By extolling grace, mercy, love, and compassion on someone in this disposition instead of judgement, avoidance, shame or even gossip...you help to bring God's love and power into the situation and open the door for even quicker healing and restoration!

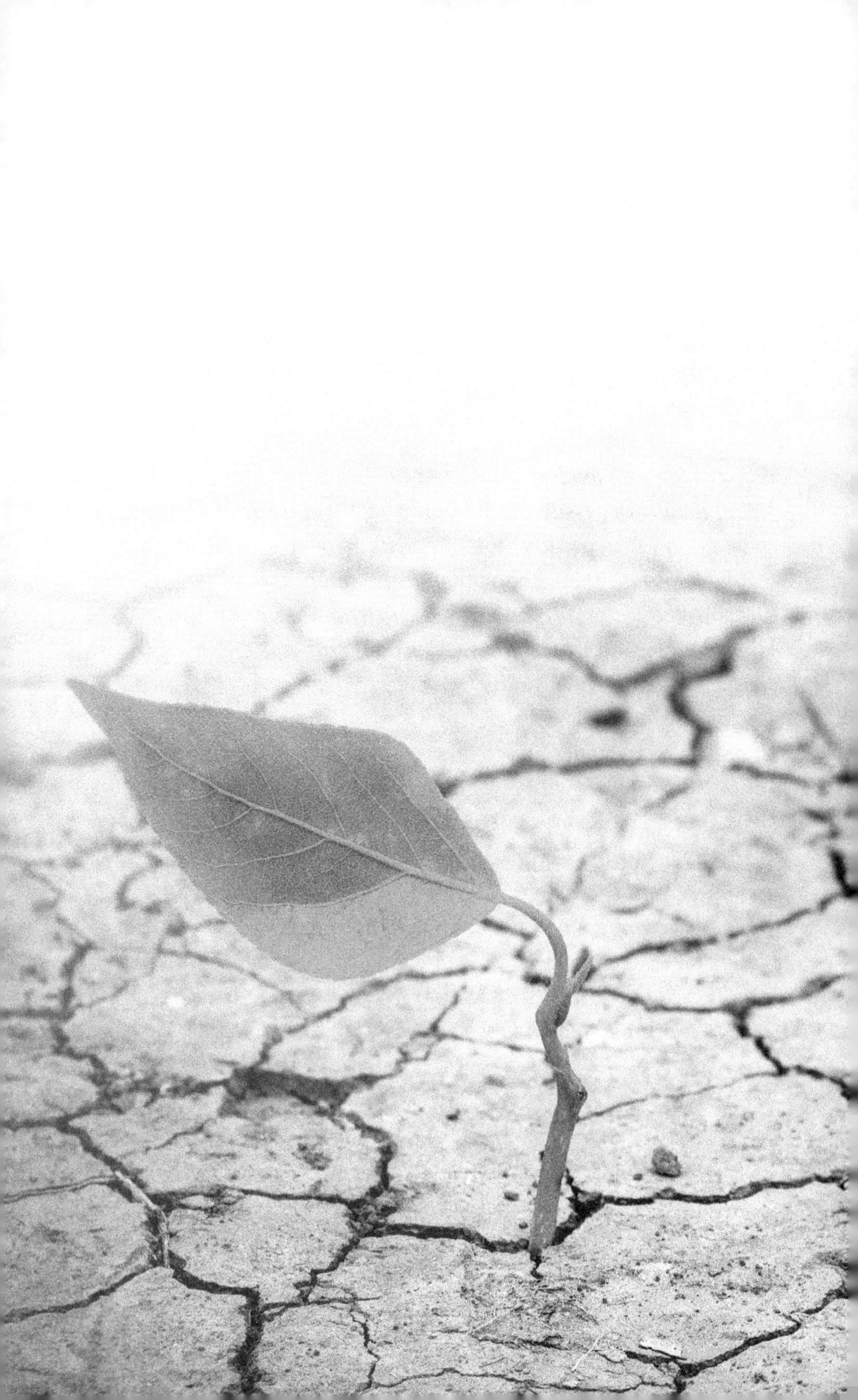

10

ON THE ROAD TO RESTORATION

I am no longer angry or bitter about the actions of my denomination nor the treatment of many folks that were once my friends in ministry. I have long since been healed from those offenses. Even those that I unfortunately never had the opportunity to go to them directly and try to resolve them between us as they have just not been accessible. That is one of the main reasons why it took so long to heal.

My wife and I were mostly healed from the damage associated with my incidence of infidelity somewhere around 5-6 years later I believe. Things had gotten progressively better all the time, but it probably took that long to almost be ready to go "partially" back into ministry. I am convinced that If you do not take enough time to totally heal you will find yourself having a setback in the midst of serving. You will think that you are healed and all a sudden a trigger or some snare that the enemy has set will offset the progress towards restoring your marriage or ministry. You can handle those attacks or setbacks much easier while healing outside of your call to ministry. If you happen to have jumped back in too early, it most likely will show up or erupt in whatever area you happen to be serving in.

So, after about five years we started to commit to a few areas of serving or volunteering. We occasionally served or volunteered in the past but nothing major or on a regular basis. Things like greeting, serving, and cleaning up after luncheons or small tasks the church needed done. Nothing too out front or long term. I personally still had an apprehension of getting too involved. I knew that I was still dealing with the most recent church offenses that came about because of my moral failure in ministry. I was able to handle a lot of abuse in past ministry positions so it was not enough to make me leave the church like it may have caused some people to do. And, I knew or understood that their poor treatment was partly the result of my own doing or failure, so I felt like I bore a share of that responsibility. Even so, I did not want to make myself vulnerable to any additional offenses that might come out of serving. I just was not ready for that.

Additionally, I also had to deal with a new and unexpected indignation. I knew that I had developed a bit of resentment surrounding the knowledge that others had seemingly profited off their immoral behaviors while I personally was subjected to devastating consequences and almost total destruction in my life. Famous or well-known individuals both inside and outside the church not only capitalized off their infidelity, but they seemed to rebound in record time. Whether it is wrong or not for me to feel that resentment; it is still a real dilemma that you probably have to go through. You may even have an idea of some of those that I am referring to. It did not seem fair to me. I knew it was a spiritual attack by the enemy because why should I care? Yet, I did have those resentful thoughts and I knew that at some point I would need to overcome them.

I am of the opinion that those public figures never fully addressed their underlying issues. Many of them have had repeated failures that would seem to support my line of thinking. Having gone through a traumatic experience like this; I am sold on the perspective that it takes somewhere around 5 years in most cases to really heal from immoral failures. Each case is undeniably different, but there is so much emotional, psychological, and spiritual damage involved that it seems ridiculous to think any differently. You simply cannot see into the future and anticipate all the potential triggers, setbacks and spiritual attacks that will indeed come into play. Those attacks will become fewer and they will have bigger gaps in between them, but they will indeed happen. And, it is not ideal or advisable for them to surface when you have prematurely entered back into ministry. Our time of healing took approximately 5 years despite the fact that we had already been happily married for close to twenty-five years and my wife was a strong believer who wholly trusted God. Thus, it may take even longer for others because I believe that we quite possibly were on the shorter end of the timeline.

I am convinced that although God does great miracles and can bring instant healing where necessary; this particular transgression with its inherent consequences takes a lot more time because of our human attributes. I am confident that He knows and understands that. If you have not fully resolved any underlying issues and healed completely, I would caution you to avoid jumping back into ministry as any unresolved issues will undoubtedly surface again later. The cliché of "once a cheater, always a cheater" most likely evolved from the instances where it has resurfaced when character or spiritual issues have not been fully addressed. Not because there is no cure for it or healing from it but because individuals have been influenced to believe that "getting back in the saddle again" was somehow a good strategy to consider.

I knew that I would need to fully resolve all of the offenses that I was still clinging on to before even thinking about ministry again. So, yes much of the delay for going any deeper after the first five years of healing was mostly on my shoulders as I slowly sought to overcome the church offenses that came about or were instigated because of my moral failure. They were new offenses where the church had either abandoned me or exhibited hurtful treatment. Thus, I was purposely reserved and careful to even consider the thought of getting too plugged in. As a matter of fact, I was almost content in the thought of never going beyond just volunteering once in a while and leaving any consideration for a return to ministry in the past.

Even though I had been able to identify all of the contributing factors in what led to my moral failure; I was actually scared to death to ever put myself close to any situation that could potentially cause the kind of damage and destruction that I experienced. Not because I was afraid of being unable to handle any future temptations to sin or worried about infidelity ever creeping back in; but because I had a personal knowledge of just how much pain and damage the enemy can inflict upon your life. I did not want any part of any more pain in my life and felt that I had less of a chance of experiencing any if I stayed out of ministry. So, I was content on just filling a pew spot. I convinced myself that I could escape most spiritual attacks if I stayed off the radar for the most part. I felt that the enemy would not have much interest in me if I just watched from the sidelines.

Many church leaders reading this book would no doubt want to encourage or exhort me to not be such a spiritual wimp. Many already have expressed that viewpoint to me. Their counsel was always based on their limited assumptions that I did not know or understand verses like "God has not given us a spirit of fear" or warnings like "pride goes before destruction and a haughty spirit before a fall." However, I knew those verses well back then and yet I still fell into a trap.

Many of us oftentimes take the power and craftiness of the enemy too lightly. Even if you ministered in the dark spiritual realm that I had done so often in the past you can still be deceived or get blindsided. I certainly was caught off guard. This was a different situation for me this time because I now had the benefit of personal experience. If you can call it a benefit because it was a very costly and devastating lesson. Since I had discovered all that went into the development of my spiritual trap, my fear wasn't so much about whether I would be able to avoid the pitfalls of developing a prideful spirit; but rather more about questioning the logic of why I would even want to place myself in another vulnerable spot like ministry. Thus, I was constantly making excuses and trying to bide as much time as much as I could. However, I knew in my spirit that I could avoid God only so long and I would eventually have to trust Him and cast all my concerns on Him. I finally made significant breakthrough in this area approximately 10 years after my fall in ministry. God gave me assurance and a release to start moving forward. It was still a bit slower than when I first dived right into ministry years ago, but it was no longer at a snail's pace.

I had this book on my heart for a long time, but I never felt a release from God to actually begin it. I had accumulated a lot of notes and the Holy Spirit continued to provide words or thoughts, but I did not have an overwhelming or compelling drive to begin. Most of it was tied to still having to completely resolve a few remaining wounds. I knew that any remaining anger or bitterness would most likely show through the content in the pages if I did not address them. Even more importantly I knew that I could not re-start in ministry and head down the same path that I had come out of with unresolved church wounds. Surely, anger and bitterness would grow into pride and resentment like it previously did. God knew that I had not resolved everything and thus I never got that release or drive to start the manuscript until nearly 10 years after my fall. It took another five years before I finally felt like I was ready, and God was behind me 100%. It had not taken this long because of Him or His unwillingness to heal me from those wounds, but because of my own reluctance towards having to revisit them.

I made tremendous progress on making my way back to being fully restored but I could only see that progress after more than a decade of healing and battling. My wife was light years ahead of me as she had healed from the infidelity long ago and kept trying to drag and prod me along. But, she did not have all the wounds and baggage that I still held on to from past ministry. She was patient and very understanding during that time, yet she really wanted to open the floodgates for more fire in her life and see me get back into ministry. I tried to show some willingness to go a little deeper by agreeing to serve in some ways that went beyond the simple things that we had volunteered for in the past. For instance, we were asked to lead a marriage series based on our testimony of what we had endured in our marriage and what they felt would help to bring others healing in their marriages. It was a popular class that was scheduled for a 6 weeks period of time which provided a great atmosphere for us to get our "feet wet" again. Nonetheless, it was also the first time I had given a testimony of what happened in our marriage since leaving full-time ministry, so it was still a bit of a stretch for me.

Most people in our new church that we had been hiding in had no idea about our past because we did a good job of just sitting amongst the crowd for the first 5 years. We continued to teach that class for a while and became involved with joining the ministry team for altar calls. Then we joined the team that facilitated bi-annual restoration seminars. They were 2-day seminars that targeted a variety of wounds that people might have in the church. Even if they did not know that they existed. Those seminars were extremely helpful in not only restoring and repairing some areas of our lives, but also were instrumental in motivating us to go deeper into serving again. We had definitely picked up the pace a bit but we both still knew how much I was holding back.

A short time later an opportunity arose to volunteer to help pioneer a new church location out of the main campus. The church had been expanding by adding new locations or campuses with a vision for expanding throughout the next 40 years. They requested a 1-year commitment from volunteers in order to establish the church and maintain some stability while growing. We committed to serving for a year, although we actually ended up staying a bit over 2 years. That was huge for us because it was the first long term commitment towards ministry that we had made in over a decade. We became the outreach coordinators while serving there and had the opportunity to impart what we had learned over the years as well as just have fun in volunteering or serving in ministry once again. It was also the first time that I preached in over 10 years as they offered me an opportunity to give a message to the young adults. It was almost as close to fully committing in serving as we used to do but, in all honesty, there was still a bit of reserved commitment or apprehension on my part.

We were visibly going deeper but we still had a way to go before obtaining that fire that we once had. Ultimately, we changed campuses because our daughter and grandkids went to a different campus. It enabled us to see them more often, but it also left us without any designated ministry so we just kind of attended services for a few months. All of a sudden, I did not particularly enjoy just blending in and not serving or dedicating some commitment to God. I did not have any church hurt any longer as all of that had finally been resolved over the last 10 years, so the apprehension had been waning. I had chosen to forgive all of those who had brought on any hurt or pain by judging or isolating me in some way. Even if I did not have the opportunity to biblically confront them.

Despite knowing that all the anger, bitterness and hurt had been taken care of; I still had some self-resistance and reservation about fully diving into any ministry even though it was indeed diminishing.

The fire and passion that had once been prevalent in my life was just not there.

I was not sure if I had just grown a little lukewarm over the years from sitting on the sidelines or if I had a confidence problem for some reason. Or perhaps, there was some other reason for my burner to still be stuck on a low flame. In some ways I felt content with staying a little hidden behind the scenes and just blending in with crowd; and yet I was starting to feel more conviction from purposefully and intentionally holding back. My excuses were falling flat, and I did not seem to have God's approval for sitting on the sidelines any longer. I knew He was telling me that I had been restored and it was time for me to start getting on track. Time to get more into the Word, time to align my personal life in preparation for ministry, time to begin this book and time to seek His direction.

My wife and I had been wrestling a bit with exactly where we were supposed to serve at the new campus that we were attending. We had found a place to just jump in and help since they needed help in the children's ministries, yet, we did not seem to have any purpose or direction on specifically what it was we were called to commit to. We could obviously do a lot of things, but I was personally wanting God to specifically provide direction. Early 2020 rolled around without still having figured anything out. Some people in the church might have been satisfied or even challenged to simply volunteer wherever and whenever needed like we have always done, but we knew God expected more from us. When I say volunteer; my wife and I are notorious for doing whatever needs to be done regardless of what area of ministry we might be serving in. We have never had the mentality or heart to ignore a need merely because "it's not our job." So, we have always naturally gone beyond just typical "volunteering" in the practical sense. We just wanted to know what God had planned and what area we needed to pursue, regardless of whether it involved just volunteering, part-time or full-time ministry.

Even though we were always rising to the occasion and helping as needed, it sometimes felt like we were still just spiritually wandering around from one opportunity of being useful to another.

However, finally after a series of unexpected events, it became apparent that the reason for the absence of direction was because we were looking in the wrong place. God was simply showing us that it was time for us to go. We had been at the church for nearly fifteen years and had spent a huge amount of that time trying to heal (and hide). The church was instrumental and gracious in helping us to heal. Although we loved the church, we knew that this had only been a transition place (a long one at that) and now it was time to prepare for the next part of our journey. The funny thing about it is that I did not have any more fear, apprehension, or reservations about re-entering ministry. I really had not even noticed that change. I was not sure what the future would hold and whether it would be continuing to volunteer, part-time ministry, or full-time ministry, but it did not matter. We were sure about very little other than we knew it was time to go and that we were ready to go where we needed to be.

So, here we are now in early 2020 and the fire inside has been ignited for both me and my wife. I cannot believe how long it took. A dramatic chain of events has all happened so quickly and collaboratively that we are both amazed at how fast God is suddenly moving in our lives.

I am sure much of it has had to do with me getting out of His way and being willing to finally leave the spiritual comfort zone that I had built around me. As well as just placing our trust all on Him.

A chain of events would indisputably and ironically lead us to go back to the church where we were that first helped us after my fall in ministry. If you asked me to guess where God was leading us, that would have been one of the furthest places that I would have had in mind. Not because of any negative experiences. Quite the contrary. Although they were great friends of ours and were of the few who did not abandon us when we needed support the most, I just figured all that was in our past. I had no idea nor had even really considered it up until God started strangely putting the pieces together.

Our pastor friends had remained friends with us for the past fifteen years from when they first let us go. They were not responsible for my fall in ministry nor any of the treatment and abuses during that time. They were there to counsel us, pray with us, and pray for us as well as pour out love on us while we went through that mess. They never tried to keep us from leaving when they knew we needed to go heal and they never tried to coax us back. We had met with them a couple of times for lunch or dinner before we ever decided to go back and quite frankly, they had no idea at the time what God was stirring in our hearts. Over the last few months, the Holy Spirit confirmed in both of our spirits that it was time to come back home. Now that it was confirmed, we could let our other church know what God was doing and that it was time to move on to the next part of our journey. I was sure they would be overjoyed as they had invested a lot in us over the years as they patiently waited and believed that God would fully restore us. And... they were!

As I finish writing this book, we do not know exactly what God has planned for us in the future other than it is time to return to our prior church home and just let Him guide us. We know that God has carefully watched over us and given us the time needed to ensure that all things had been healed and restored. Including the fire in our spirits that had somehow evaded us or had been doused for so long. We are extremely confident that we are indeed called to be there to serve and support our friends in whatever way that God wants us to. And, I just recently got back my credentials from the new denomination that they are under. Unbelievably, the denomination has a heart for restoring pastors and leaders and that which the enemy has tried to steal from so many men and women of God. I never thought that would happen again to be honest with you. This time though it is not for the sake of a title... It is just an establishment of credibility and accountability to let me return to filling the role as an evangelist. That which I was called to do. We now know that exciting times lay ahead, and that full restoration has finally taken place full-circle!

CONCLUSION

This book was extremely difficult to write. It took many years to complete and the wounds that re-surfaced or were uncovered were evidence of further healing needed each time that I attempted to complete it. The evidence or presence of those wounds let me know that I was not fully healed or restored and that they needed to be resolved first. That caused many setbacks over a long period of time. I am extremely grateful for the patience of God and the patience of those who poured into me and my wife's lives in the past 15 years. Were it not for that, I would no doubt still be impacted by past wounds and could have possibly become just another church statistic.

Although some Church offenses are undoubtedly just perceived offenses, I believe the vast majority of them are legitimate. They cause real pain and real damage to people both emotionally and spiritually. As my book illustrates…they do not just happen to members or regular attendees of the church but to leaders and pastors as well. I have known so many pastors and leaders that have been wounded over the years that are no longer serving in ministry after having sustained what seems to be irreparable harm. Ministry is extremely rewarding, but it can also seem brutal at times. It involves working relationships with people or imperfect human beings, so unfortunately you will not always be treated with the respect, decency or love that should come from Christians. It may even cause you to consider the thought that "no wonder why those outside the church take issue with the church and Christians in general." If you have served in ministry and experienced church offenses while serving; unfortunately, you are not alone.

The good news is that God is faithful. Some of those trials or tribulations will help to mold or fortify you going forward. Even though they are not pleasant to go through. If you have not fully healed yet or been fully restored, you may need more time than you thought you would. It took me close to 15 years overall. I partially re-entered ministry during that time, but it took that long for complete restoration. Some of that was due to my own resistance because of the nature and severity of everything involved with my personal experiences, but it was certainly longer than I anticipated or thought. I pray it does not take that long for you if you are reading this book and wondering just how long it will take for you. Just know that God is patient with you but at some point, He will want you to move beyond your scars.

In closing, there are a few critical and highlighted points that I want to make in order to bring the content of this book into perspective for you. First if you are a pastor or leader inside the church, I hope that you are inspired to ask those hard questions about how you and your church might be subject to creating offenses. And, how those offenses affect the Church body or the church as a whole. The counterpart to this book *Surviving Religion: How religion is hurting the church* is my book expressly designed to help you further analyze this issue and implement the concepts and truths as a teaching series in your church. Hopefully, you develop an awareness that causes you to ponder just how many people possibly leave the church because of offenses. They may not be as strong, equipped or supported as much as my wife and I were. Losing anyone in the church (whether they are a leader of a ministry or not) does not benefit the church.

Sadly, Christians do hurt other Christians. You may want to ask yourself "how well do you support other leaders or pastors that God has placed you over?" Do you support them or oppose them? Positions of leadership in the church should exemplify God's character and be approached with humility, fairness, truth, wisdom, grace, mercy, and love in mind. They are not for the purpose of or displaying or abusing power and authority over others. God is ultimately in control of the church and the facilitation of church business. Spiritual growth in the church and others should always be under His direction.

Ministry presents some extraordinary sacrifices and hardships on the individuals and their families that are willing to enter into it. Many of them have to work outside of the church in addition to serving in order to financially provide for their families. Most have invested a good portion of their life just to help and serve others. As a leader do you consider the sacrifices that ministry leaders make before criticizing them? Do you honor their spouses who are "partners" with them regardless of whether they have a title, are on the payroll or out in front of the congregation? Do you earnestly pray for them and seek ways to support or encourage them? You may want to ask God to show you where you may fall short in being supportive of those people in ministry or ways to go beyond what you currently offer them. Be thankful that someone is willing to sacrifice and serve the body.

Alongside the consideration of what your church is doing to address or reduce the number of church offenses is the question of what are you doing about the "impact" of them on the Church body? Do you specifically offer opportunities for individuals in your church to examine and seek healing for church hurts? This includes new members or attendees who may be carrying some of that baggage with them. You cannot assume that all your visitors or "solid" additions do not have some past offense that remains unresolved as it can affect your church. I know of several churches that offer counseling, restoration seminars or classes specifically to address these issues and have found great success in doing so. I wrote the book *Surviving Religion: How Religion is hurting the church* and designed it for those purposes along with a handbook to help facilitate restorative classes. I would encourage you to consider some of these kinds of options and not take the problem of church offenses and wounds lightly or the healthiness of your church for granted if you do not yet have anything else in place.

Secondly, if you are someone who has been unfortunately impacted by something as traumatic as infidelity you should understand that recovering from something like that is a long and arduous process. It is not any worse than any other sin in God's eyes, but it does unfortunately possess extraordinary consequences. If you are an unfortunate party to this in some way you may be asking just how much damage does it cause and how much time does it take to heal or be restored? The quick and simple answer is "a lot." However, you can be fully healed and fully restored. God is faithful no matter how long it may take.

Moral failures are difficult circumstances whether you are a pastor or not. It is not an easy undertaking to fight for your marriage, but it is certainly worth fighting for. I cannot guarantee you that it will work out 100% to your expectations, but I can tell you that God will be with you the entire time if you let Him. If you are in ministry then you are probably wondering if you will ever be able to return to it. Or, maybe you have already determined that you do not want to return because of your vulnerability and possible shame. I know that I personally questioned myself and all the good things I did in ministry. I had literally led thousands of individuals to the Lord over time and yet I wondered after my fall if it was all a sham on my part or all for nothing. Was my character and integrity all a joke or was this an isolated incident? Be cognizant of the fact that the enemy does not want you to go back into ministry or be a productive member of the body and he will do everything possible to keep you from it. It will be painful, and you will need to address "all" unresolved hurts or issues, but I am sure that God does want you to go back to your calling and serving others. He will provide a way if you hang in there. No matter how long it takes.

You may be wondering if you will ever be able to forget such an experience like moral failures. The unequivocal answer is "no" and you would be foolish for trying to claim such. Both of you will always have scars. As a matter of fact, it is doubtful that you will be able to forget many of the other church offenses either. Forgetting is not the same as forgiving. Wounds produce scabs and scabs once they heal produce scars. It will always be there. But the scar will fade over time and should serve as a positive reminder of how God brought you through all of the pain and hurt of a wound before it became a mere scar.

I have found that many pastors and leaders are ill-equipped to effectively counsel or handle matters associated with infidelity. They should seek advisement or help for matters that go beyond their level of experience or area of expertise. Relying on their own intellect will not sufficiently replace relying on God and approaching matters like this with a sense of humility that acknowledges their limited knowledge or wisdom in some areas. They should also seek to be as patient as God is with us instead of trying to force people to heal or operating on their own timeline. They should avoid trying to address this topic profoundly from the pulpit if they have no real idea what they are talking about or are in way over their head. You need to turn to the Holy Spirit and ask for guidance and the right balance between sensitivity and conveying the biblical truths surrounding it. Not everyone is overly sensitive and to those who have gone through it, they will know just how ignorant that you are on the subject.

Thirdly, in light of the experiences that I provided for you that my wife and I encountered throughout the course of serving in ministry, some of you may wonder…" how do you handle controlling or difficult leadership?" Will simply praying about it resolve things? How much do you endure or how long do you stay before leaving? Those are great questions for which my wife and I do not have a profound or absolute answer for. We were probably able to endure more than many folks and yet maybe not as much as others could have. I could tell you that you have to wait until God tells you it is time to leave but even that can be difficult to figure out as well. I have often wondered if we had waited too long to leave in some instances. I do know however that you need to be careful so that staying does not damage your family or your own spiritual condition. And… please be careful to properly assess whether your leadership really is controlling or difficult instead of the issue just being a few disagreements or maybe even something that you share at least part of the blame in. There needs to be a definitive pattern in their behaviors and not just some isolated mistakes, misunderstandings, or differing views.

Fourthly, it is extremely possible that just about anyone reading this book may have some unresolved church offense that needs to be addressed. Just because it is hidden or has been for many years does not mean that it does not still exist. Overcoming church offenses is going to take some level of forgiveness on your part and some spiritual healing and restoration from God. You may not be able to face or discuss the offense with some of those who initiated it but you will still need to earnestly and honestly take it before God in order for the spiritual aspects to be purged and authentically repaired.

Many church offenses can be somewhat easily and quickly resolved. Others that are more damaging may take more time, maybe counseling, lots of prayer and progressive healing. However, you should know that God is patient and faithful, so I am confident that you will indeed find the restoration that you are seeking. God loves you and wants everyone to be a part of the body. He wants you to be an active contributor that is not isolated or separated from the rest of the Church. So, make a personal commitment in staying connected to the Church and remaining focused on Him in order to take hold of the blessed and joy-filled life that He desires for you. Do not be robbed of it through an unresolved church offense that still causes anger, pain, bitterness, and resentment. Even if you do not see it or think that it does not exist any longer merely because time has passed.

Lastly, you should know that no ministry or church is perfect. Neither the human beings that lead them nor the people that you serve are perfect. I can almost guarantee you that you will have some good times and you will have some bad experiences. Most likely the bad times will not last forever. Make an extra effort to remember all the good things that happen because I am sure that they will undoubtedly overshadow the bad experiences no matter how difficult any of them might be to overcome. As I wrote this book it surprisingly reminded me of even more good times than I could recollect. And, all the people and souls that were impacted. You may have to heal from some wounds but do not let the enemy steal your joy that could keep you from doing the very things you love and were called to do.

REFERENCES

Introduction

James C. Jones. *Surviving Religion: How religion is hurting the church*. Surviving Religion: How religion is hurting the Church. 2020

1 COR 12:12-31 (Holy Bible: New International Version; all subsequent citations from this same version unless otherwise noted).

Chapter 1 Believe me; I know

George Barna. Churchless: Understanding Today's Unchurched and How to connect with Them. Tyndale Momentum. Carol Stream, IL. 2016.

https://christianchronicle.org/church-in-decline-u-s-culture-to-blame/

https://www.schwartzreport.net/7-startling-facts-an-up-close-look-at-church-attendance-in-america/

https://churchleaders.com/pastors/pastor-articles/139575-7-startling-facts-an-up-close-look-at-church-attendance-in-america.html

http://nationalblackroberegiment.com/shocking-statistics-church-decline/

www.barna.com/research/church-attendance-trends

https://factsandtrends.net/2018/12/17/the-number-1-reason-for-the-decline-in-church-attendance/

https://www.pewforum.org/2019/10/17/in-u-s-decline-of-christianity-continues-at-rapid-pace/https://www.barna.com/research/changing-state-of-the-church/

https://news.gallup.com/poll/248837/church-membership-down-sharply-past-two-decades.aspx

https://www.barna.com/research/americans-divided-on-the-importance-of-church/

https://www.barna.com/research/five-trends-among-the-unchurched/

https://www.christianitytoday.com/karl-vaters/2018/may/church-attendance-patterns-are-changing-we-have-to-adapt.html

https://simpletexting.com/increase-church-attendance/

https://churchmojo.com/2016/11/29/church-attendance/

JHN 10:10

Chapter 2 A Cracked but Firm Foundation

The Marriage Group. (2017). A Brief History of Marriage: 1960's to present. Retrieved February 19, 2020. https://themarriage-group.com/brief-history-marriage-1960s-present/

PRO 22:6

National Institute on Drug Abuse. Drugs, Brains and Behaviors. Retrieved on January 31, 2020. https://www.drugabuse.gov/publications/drugs-brains-behavior-science-addiction/drug-misuse-addiction

ROM 8:28

Chapter 3 Living a Lifestyle of Least Resistance

explanatorytexts.com/path-of-least-resistance/#:~:text=The%20chemist%20Le%20Chatelier%20first%20used%20the%20term,opposition%2C%20it%20follows%20the%20path%20of%20least%20resistance.

1 SAM 13:14; ACT 13:22

Chapter 4 Call to Ministry

Wiki. List of Religious Slurs. Retrieved online March 1, 2020. https://abuse.wikia.org/wiki/List_of_religious_slurs

Greg Laurie. The Invisible World. First Edition. 1991. FMG Distribution, Newport Beach, CA.

Christian History. The Praise and Worship Revolution. Retrieved April 2, 2020. https://www.christianitytoday.com/history/2008/october/praise-and-worship-revolution.html

Church Leaders. The stumbling blocks to Church Change. Retrieved April 2, 2020. https://churchleaders.com/pastors/pastor-articles/145209-stumbling-blocks-to-church-change.html

JAS 1:22

PSA 119:11

EPH 4:11

Chapter 5 The Early Challenges in Ministry

https://www.biblestudytools.com/bible-study/topical-studies/can-women-be-pastors.html

https://carm.org/should-women-be-pastors-and-elders

Grunge. The Editors of Encyclopaedia Britannica. Retrieved April 3, 2020. https://www.britannica.com/art/grunge-music

Neil T. Anderson. Victory Over The Darkness. Regal Books. 1990. Ventura, CA.

JAS 1:22

2TIM 1:7

Christian Century. "Just As I Am," Billy Graham's signature hymn, embodied his style as an evangelist. https://www.christian-century.org/blog-post/guest-post/just-i-am-billy-grahams-signature-hymn-embodied-his-style-evangelist

Cooper Adams. Bible Truth. The apocryphal Books. https://www.bible-truth.org/Apocrypha.html

MAT 4:19

1COR 10:13

Chapter 6 Wonder Years

Loren Mead. A Change of Pastors...and How it Affects Change in the Congregationhttps://www.amazon.com/kindle-dbs/hz/subscribe/ku?pd_rd_w=Mh6HE&pd_rd_wg=PvNmF&pd_rd_r=ab1b502b-b76b-4fd1-8e77-e61b6410caf7&shoppingPortalEnabled=true

HOS 14.6, EXD 30:34-38

ACT 2:1-12; 1COR 12; 1COR 14

MAT 3:11; ACT 1:5; ACT 1:8; ACT 2:38; ACT 4:31: ROM 8:9-11; 1COR 12; 1COR 14

JHN 16:8; EPH 2:8

Chapter 7 The Good, the Bad and the Ugly
ROM 8:28

Charles Dickens. Richard Maxwell (Editor). 30th Edition. Bantam Classics. 1985. Tale of Two Cities.

Chapter 8 Pride Goes Before Destruction

JHN 2:14; MAT 21:12-13; MAR 3:5; PSA 7:11; EPH 4:26-27; EXD 4:14; EXD 22:21-24, NUM 11:1, 10; NUM 12:9.

https://fliphtml5.com/kgcw/hwpg/basic

Chapter 9 The Unpardonable Sin
GEN 2:24

MRK 3:22-30; MAT 12:22-32

EXD 20: 1-20

Chapter 10 On the Road to Restoration
PRO 16:18, 2TIM 1:7

1PET 5:7

ROM 3:23; ROM 6:23; JAS 2:10; JAS 4:17

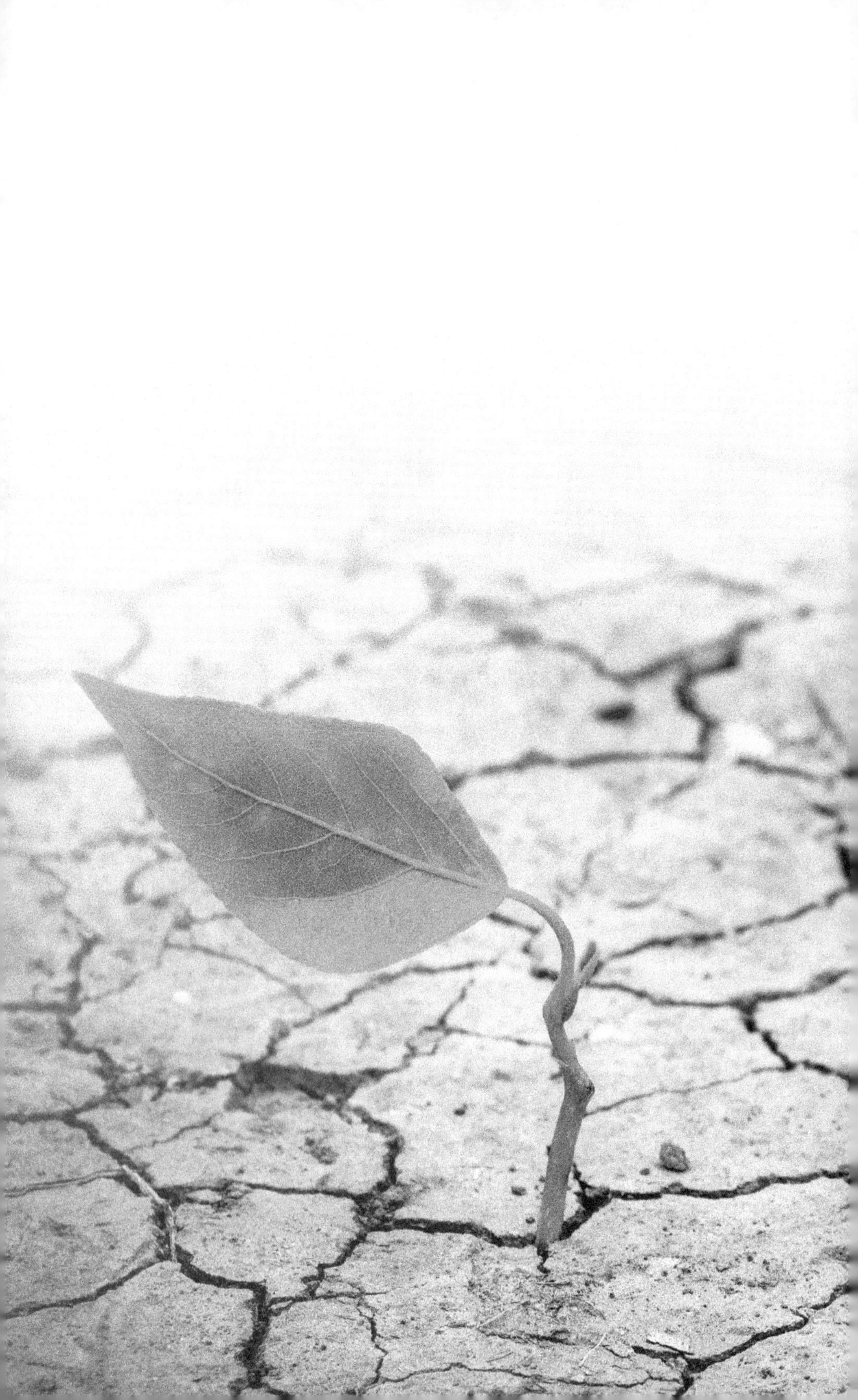

NOTE FROM SUSAN:

When the Lord calls your spouse to the ministry it is not just them that He calls, but it is you as well in answering our Heavenly Father's request to serve others. You become partners in ministry! Jim and I heard Him loud and clear, but when we started off on our journey, we had no idea what all that would entail. Naturally, we thought every opportunity to serve would be positive with doors flying open for us to walk through with welcoming arms. But reality kicked us in the head and gave us a rude awakening that proved that it does not always work out that way or go that smoothly.

There were repetitive peaks and valleys that we had to venture through, but it was in those valley's where we found our greatest lessons... the breaking and building of personal character as well as the hit-home realization that God's Word is true and infallible. Though it did not always seem that way; He will never leave us nor forsake us.

I wish that we did not have to go through all the pain and necessary healing that would come about from life lessons while in the valleys; but they are life lessons that made us who we are today. Many of those were uninvited consequences that we brought upon ourselves from our own choices or decisions, but God still used them to mold us, build us and restore us. I love who we are today!

We are now both strong oak trees with roots that grow deep and are founded in God's unfailing love and faithfulness in our lives. This has helped us to be relational and compassionate to others that find themselves having to endure the many trials that we also found ourselves in.

As humans we are not perfect, but we are in pursuit of the one who is. His name is Jesus.

If you don't know Jesus Christ as your personal Savior; the One that you can cast all your cares on so that you can walk in triumphant boldness, we would love to help you in knowing Him. He Loves YOU! And He wants nothing more than to spend time with you. Please allow Him to enter your heart, restore what has been broken and give you back the joy, because it is by faith you stand firm!

I love you my friend,
Susan